WHO PUT JESUS ON THE CROSS

A.W. TOZER

WHO PUT JESUS ON THE CROSS

**Twelve messages on
Well-known and favorite
Bible texts**

Edited and Compiled
by Gerald B. Smith

christian publications, inc.

25 South Tenth Street, Harrisburg, Pa. 17101

The Mark of *CP* Vibrant Faith

Printed in the United States of America

Contents

Preface

Those who were friends and associates of Dr. A. W. Tozer during his lifetime knew of his very strong convictions against any kind of false profession or "phony" attitudes in the Christian life and ministry.

The reader of these sermons will note in several chapters the manner in which Dr. Tozer was willing to bare his own soul in affirmation of Christian honesty, candor and transparency among ministers and laymen alike.

In the chapter, "What Is It Costing You to Be a Christian?", Dr. Tozer asked his congregation to pray for him and the integrity of his ministry:

> *"Pray that I will not just come to a wearied end —an exhausted, tired, old preacher, interested only in hunting a place to roost. Pray that I will let my Christian standards cost me something right down to the last gasp!"*

He never lost that insistent spirit on behalf of genuineness and truth. Just a few weeks before his unexpected death in 1963, Dr. Tozer was asked by an official of the National Association of Evangelicals to address the annual convention of the NAE in Buffalo, New York.

Because he had not been a proponent of Christian and Missionary Alliance membership in the NAE, Dr. Tozer asked frankly:

"Do you think I have something to contribute to your meeting—or are you just trying to 'butter' me up?"

Assured of the integrity of the invitation, Dr. Tozer consented and gave a memorable address on Christian commitment to the NAE convention delegates. It was his last public address and presentation of the claims of Christ outside of his own pulpit prior to his death in May 1963.

The Publisher

Chapter One

Who Put Jesus on the Cross?

"He was wounded for our transgressions, he was bruised for our iniquities: the chastisement of our peace was upon him; and with his stripes we are healed." Isaiah 53:5

There is a strange conspiracy of silence in the world today—even in religious circles—about man's responsibility for sin, the reality of judgment, and about an outraged God and the necessity for a crucified Saviour.

On the other hand, there is an open and powerful movement swirling throughout the world designed to give people peace of mind in relieving them of any historical responsibility for the trial and crucifixion of Jesus Christ. The problem with modern decrees and pronouncements in the name of brotherhood and tolerance is their basic misconception of Christian theology.

A great shadow lies upon every man and every woman—the fact that our Lord was bruised and wounded and crucified for the entire human race. This is the basic human responsibility that men are trying to push off and evade.

Let us not eloquently blame Judas nor Pilate. Let us not curl our lips at Judas and accuse, "He sold Him for money!"

Let us pity Pilate, the weak-willed, because he did not have courage enough to stand for the innocency of the man whom he declared had done no wrong.

Let us not curse the Jews for delivering Jesus to be crucified. Let us not single out the Romans in blaming them for putting Jesus on the cross.

Oh, they were guilty, certainly! But they were our accomplices in crime. They and we put Him on the cross, not they alone. That rising malice and anger that burns so hotly in your breast today put Him there. That basic dishonesty that comes to light in your being when you knowingly cheat and chisel on your income tax return—that put Him on the cross. The evil, the hatred, the suspicion, the jealousy, the lying tongue, the carnality, the fleshly love of pleasure—all of these in natural man joined in putting Him on the cross.

We may as well admit it. Every one of us in Adam's race had a share in putting Him on the cross!

I have often wondered how any professing Christian man or woman could approach the communion table and participate in the memorial of our Lord's death without feeling and sensing the pain and the shame of the inward confession: "I, too, am among those who helped put Him on the cross!"

I remind you that it is characteristic of the natural man to keep himself so busy with unimportant trifles that he is able to avoid the settling of the most important matters relating to life and existence.

Men and women will gather anywhere and everywhere to talk about and discuss every subject from the latest fashions on up to Plato and philosophy—up and down the scale. They talk about the necessity for peace. They may talk about the church and how it can be a bulwark against communism. None of these things are embarrassing subjects.

But the conversation all stops and the taboo of silence becomes effective when anyone dares to suggest that there are spiritual subjects of vital importance to our souls that ought to be discussed and considered. There seems to be an unwritten rule in polite society that if any religious subjects are to be discussed, it must be within the framework of theory—"never let it get personal!"

All the while, there is really only one thing that is of vital and lasting importance—the fact that our Lord Jesus Christ "was wounded for our transgressions; he was bruised for our iniquities; the chastisement of our peace was upon him; and with his stripes we are healed."

There are two very strong and terrible words here—*transgressions* and *iniquities*.

A *transgression* is a breaking away, a revolt from just authority. In all of the moral universe, only man and the fallen angels have rebelled and violated the authority of God, and men are still in flagrant rebellion against that authority.

There is no expression in the English language which can convey the full weight and force of terror inherent in the words *transgression* and *iniquity*. But in man's fall and transgression against the created order and authority of God we recognize perversion and twistedness and deformity and crookedness and rebellion. These are all there, and, undeniably, they reflect the reason and the necessity for the death of Jesus Christ on the cross.

The word *iniquity* is not a good word—and God knows how we hate it! But the consequences of iniquity cannot be escaped.

The prophet reminds us clearly that the Saviour was bruised for "our iniquities."

We deny it and say, "No!" but the fingerprints of all mankind are plain evidence against us. The authorities have no trouble finding and apprehending the awkward burglar who leaves his fingerprints on tables and doorknobs, for they have his record. So, the fingerprints of man are found in every dark cellar

11

and in every alley and in every dimly-lighted evil place throughout the world—every man's fingerprints are recorded and God knows man from man. It is impossible to escape our guilt and place our moral responsibilities upon someone else. It is a highly personal matter—"our iniquities."

For our iniquities and our transgressions He was bruised and wounded. I do not even like to tell you of the implications of His wounding. It really means that He was profaned and broken, stained and defiled. He was Jesus Christ when men took Him into their evil hands. Soon He was humiliated and profaned. They plucked out His beard. He was stained with His own blood, defiled with earth's grime. Yet He accused no one and He cursed no one. He was Jesus Christ, the wounded one.

Israel's great burden and amazing blunder was her judgment that this wounded one on the hillside beyond Jerusalem was being punished for His own sin.

The prophet foresaw this historic error in judgment, and he himself was a Jew, saying: "We thought He was smitten of God. We thought that God was punishing Him for His own iniquity for we did not know then that God was punishing Him for our transgressions and our iniquities."

He was profaned for our sakes. He who is the second person of the Godhead was not only wounded for us, but He was profaned by ignorant and unworthy men.

Isaiah reported that "the chastisement of our peace was upon him."

How few there are who realize that it is this peace—the health and prosperity and welfare and safety of the individual—which restores us to God. A chastisement fell upon Him so that we as individual humans could experience peace with God if we so desired. But the chastisement was upon Him. Rebuke, discipline and correction—these are found in chastisement. He was beaten and scourged in public by the decree of the Romans. They lashed Him in public view as they later lashed Paul. They whipped and punished Him in full view of the jeering public, and His bruised and bleeding and swollen person was the answer to the peace of the world and to the peace of the human heart. He was chastised for our peace; the blows fell upon Him.

I do not suppose there is any more humiliating punishment ever devised by mankind than that of whipping and flogging grown men in public view. Many men who have been put in a jail have become a kind of hero in the eye of the public. Heavy fines have been assessed against various offenders of the law, but it is not unusual for such an offender to boast and brag about his escape. But when a bad man is taken out before a laughing, jeering crowd, stripped to the waist and soundly whipped like a child—a bad child—he loses face and has no boasting left. He will probably never be the bold, bad man he was before. That kind of whipping and chastisement breaks the spirit and humiliates. The chagrin is worse than the lash that falls on the back.

I speak for myself as a forgiven and justified sinner, and I think I speak for a great host of forgiven and born-again men and women, when I say that in our repentance we sensed just a fraction and just a token of the wounding and chastisement which fell upon Jesus Christ as He stood in our place and in our behalf. A truly penitent man who has realized the enormity of his sin and rebellion against God senses a violent revulsion against himself—he does not feel that he can actually dare to ask God to let him off. But peace has been established, for the blows have fallen on Jesus Christ—publicly humiliated and disgraced as a common thief, wounded and bruised and bleeding under the lash for sins He did not commit; for rebellions in which He had no part;

13

for iniquity in the human stream that was an outrage to a loving God and Creator.

Isaiah sums up his message of a substitutionary atonement with the good news that "with his stripes we are healed."

The meaning of these "stripes" in the original language is not a pleasant description. It means to be actually hurt and injured until the entire body is black and blue as one great bruise. Mankind has always used this kind of bodily laceration as a punitive measure. Society has always insisted upon the right to punish a man for his own wrong-doing. The punishment is generally suited to the nature of the crime. It is a kind of revenge—society taking vengeance against the person who dared flout the rules.

But the suffering of Jesus Christ was not punitive. It was not for Himself and not for punishment of anything that He Himself had done.

The suffering of Jesus was corrective. He was willing to suffer in order that He might correct us and perfect us, so that His suffering might not begin and end in suffering, but that it might begin in suffering and end in healing.

Brethren, that is the glory of the cross! That is the glory of the kind of sacrifice that was for so long in the heart of God! That is the glory of the kind of atonement that allows a repentant sinner to come into peaceful and gracious fellowship with his God and Creator! It began in His suffering and it ended in our healing. It began in His wounds and ended in our purification. It began in His bruises and ended in our cleansing.

What is our repentance? I discover that repentance is mainly remorse for the share we had in the revolt that wounded Jesus Christ, our Lord. Further, I have discovered that truly repentant men never quite get over it, for repentance is not a state of mind and spirit that takes its leave as soon as God has given forgiveness and as soon as cleansing is realized.

That painful and acute conviction that accompanies repentance may well subside and a sense of peace and cleansing come, but even the holiest of justified men will think back over his part in the wounding and the chastisement of the Lamb of God. A sense of shock will still come over him. A sense of wonder will remain—wonder that the Lamb that was wounded should turn His wounds into the cleansing and forgiveness of one who wounded Him.

This brings to mind a gracious moving in many of our evangelical church circles—a willingness to move toward the spiritual purity of heart taught and exemplified so well by John Wesley in a time of spiritual dryness.

In spite of the fact that the word *sanctification* is a good Bible word, we have experienced a period in which evangelical churches hardly dared breathe the word because of the fear of being classified among the "holy rollers."

Not only is the good word *sanctification* coming back, but I am hopeful that what the word stands for in the heart and mind of God is coming back, too. The believing Christian, the child of God, should have a holy longing and desire for the pure heart and clean hands that are a delight to his Lord. It was for this that Jesus Christ allowed Himself to be humiliated, maltreated, lacerated. He was bruised, wounded and chastised so that the people of God could be a cleansed and spiritual people—in order that our minds might be pure and our thoughts pure. This provision all began in His suffering and ends in our cleansing. It began with His open, bleeding wounds and ends in peaceful hearts and calm and joyful demeanor in His people.

Every humble and devoted believer in Jesus Christ must have his own periods of wonder and amazement at this mystery of godliness—the willingness of the Son of Man to take our place in judgment and in punishment. If the amazement has all gone out of it, something is wrong, and you need to have the stony ground broken up again!

I often remind you that Paul, one of the holiest men who ever lived, was not ashamed of his times of remembrance and wonder over the grace and kindness of God. He knew that God did not hold his old sins against him forever. Knowing the account was all settled, Paul's happy heart assured him again and again that all was well. At the same time, Paul could only shake his head in amazement, and confess: "I am unworthy to be called, but by His grace, I am a new creation in Jesus Christ!"

I make this point about the faith and assurance and rejoicing of Paul in order to say that if that humble sense of perpetual penance ever leaves our justified being, we are on the way to backsliding.

Charles Finney, one of the greatest of all of God's men throughout the years, testified that in the midst of his labors and endeavors in bringing men to Christ, he would at times sense a coldness in his own heart.

Finney did not excuse it. In his writings he told of having to turn from all of his activities, seeking God's face and Spirit anew in fasting and prayer.

"I plowed up until I struck fire and met God," he wrote. What a helpful and blessed formula for the concerned children of God in every generation!

Those who compose the Body of Christ, His church, must be inwardly aware of two basic facts if we are to be joyfully effective for our Lord.

We must have the positive knowledge that we are clean through His wounds, with God's peace realized through His stripes. This is how God assures us that we may be all right inside. In this spiritual condition, we will treasure the purity of His cleansing and we will not excuse any evil or wrong-doing.

Also, we must keep upon us a joyful and compelling sense of gratitude for the bruised and wounded One, our Lord Jesus Christ. Oh, what a mystery of redemption—that the bruises of One healed the bruises of many; that the wounds of One healed the wounds of millions; that the stripes of One healed the stripes of many.

The wounds and bruises that should have fallen upon us fell upon Him, and we are saved for His sake!

Many years ago, an historic group of Presbyterians were awed by the wonder and the mystery of Christ's having come in the flesh to give Himself as an offering for every man's sin.

Those humble Christians said to one another: "Let us walk softly and search our hearts and wait on God and seek His face throughout the next three months. Then we will come to the communion table with our hearts prepared—lest the table of our Lord should become a common and careless thing."

God still seeks humble, cleansed and trusting hearts through which to reveal His divine power and grace and life. A professional botanist from the university can describe the acacia bush of the desert better than Moses could ever do—but God is still looking for the humble souls who are not satisfied until God speaks with the divine fire in the bush.

A research scientist could be employed to stand and tell us more about the elements and properties found in bread and wine than the apostles ever knew. But this is our danger: we may have lost the light and warmth of the Presence of God, and we may have only bread and wine. The fire will have gone from the bush, and the glory will not be in our act of communion and fellowship.

It is not so important that we know all of the history and all of the scientific facts, but it is vastly important that we desire and know and cherish the Presence of the Living God, who has given Jesus Christ to be the propitiation for our sins; and not for ours only, but also for the sins of the whole world.

Chapter Two

Are There Shortcuts to the Beauty of Holiness?

"Awake, O north wind; and come, thou south; blow upon my garden, that the spices thereof may flow out. Let my beloved come into his garden, and eat his pleasant fruits." Song of Solomon 4:16

I would like to be able to ask every Christian in the world this question: "Are you really interested in God's producing in you the beautiful fruits and fragrances of the Holy Ghost?"

For every affirmative answer, I would quickly recommend:

Then look to your own willingness to be regular in the habits of a holy life—for flowers and fruit do not grow in thin air! They grow and come up out of a root and "the root of the righteous yieldeth fruit."

For every beautiful garden that you see, whose fragrance comes out to welcome you, has its roots down into the hard earth. The beautiful flowers and blooms will grow and appear and flourish only when there are deep roots and strong stalks. If you take the roots away, the blossom and flower will endure perhaps one day. The sun will scorch them and they will be gone.

Now, we Christians, for the most part, reserve most of our interest for the fruit and the spice and

18

the beauty of the garden. Most of us go to church, I think, for the same simple reason that a child climbs into its mother's arms after a long day at play, with many falls and bumps and frights and disappointments. The child wants consolation.

It appears that most people go to church for consolation. In fact, we have now fallen upon times when religion is mostly for consolation. We are now in the grip of the cult of peace—peace of mind, peace of heart, peace of soul, and we want to relax and have the great God Almighty pat our heads and comfort us. This has become religion.

This, along with one other item: the threat that if you don't be good the nuclear bomb will wipe out your modern civilization!

These seem to be the only two motives that remain in the wide world for religion. If you are not good, they warn, civilization will fall apart and the bomb will get us all, and if you do not come to the Lord, you will never have peace!

So, between fear and the desire to be patted and chucked under the chin and cuddled, the professing Christian staggers along his way.

My brethren, there is something better than this, something that has roots.

According to my Bible, there should be a people of God—they do not all have to belong to one church—but there should be a people called out by the Lord God and subjected to a spiritual experience given by God. Then they are to learn to walk in the way of the Truth and the way of the scriptures, producing the righteous fruit of the child of God whatever world conditions may be.

They know that those who destroy the body are not important—only those who destroy the soul. You can disintegrate a man, a saint of God, with a bomb and he is in heaven immediately with his Lord. The enemies of God have slain many Christians and sent them off quickly to be with God. They cast their bodies aside as unclean things, but the souls of those men and women were immediately with the Lord.

Then there is the matter of constant consolation and peace—the promise of always feeling relaxed and at rest and enjoying ourselves inwardly.

This, I say, has been held up as being quite the proper goal to be sought in the evil hour in which we live. We forget that our Lord was a man of sorrow and acquainted with grief. We forget the arrows of grief and pain which went through the heart of Jesus' mother, Mary. We forget that all of the apostles except John died a martyr's death. We forget that there were 13 million Christians slain during the first two generations of the Christian era. We forget that they languished in prison, that they were starved, were thrown over cliffs, were fed to the lions, were drowned, that they were sewn in sacks and thrown into the ocean.

Yes, we want to forget that most of God's wonderful people in the early days of the church did not have peace of mind. They did not seek it. They knew that a soldier does not go to the battlefield to relax— he goes to fight. They accepted their position on earth as soldiers in the army of God, fighting along with the Lord Jesus Christ in the terrible war against iniquity and sin. It was not a war against people but against sin and iniquity and the devil!

There was much distress, many heartaches, painful bruises, flowing tears, much loss and many deaths.

But there is something better than being comfortable, and the followers of Christ ought to find it out— the poor, soft, overstuffed Christians of our time ought to find it out! There is something better than being comfortable!

We Protestants have forgotten altogether that there is such a thing as discipline and suffering. We live within an economy that enables us to have plenty. We live under a political system that enables us to believe anything we want or nothing at all and still not be in trouble with the law. The result is that we have concocted a religion of sweet wine which we drink eagerly in the hope that we can walk around in a state of pleasant intoxication.

Now is that what God really wants to do for men and women?

No. God wants to bring us the fruit of the Spirit— love, joy, peace, longsuffering, gentleness, goodness, faith, meekness and temperance. The apostle Paul made it very plain in his language to the Ephesians that God wants to do something within every one of us that will cause us to love everybody, letting all bitterness and wrath and clamour and evil speaking be put away from among us, assuring that we will be kind to one another, tenderhearted, forgiving one another, even as God has, for Christ's sake, forgiven us.

That is what God wants to do: to bring out the likeness of Christ in the heart and life of the redeemed man. That is the purpose of God—not to make him happy, although in that condition he is likely to be happy. Not to make his civilization safe, although if there are enough people like that in the world, civilization has a better chance to survive.

So, this is our difficulty, brethren. We try to arrive at the fruits of Christianity by a shortcut. Of course, everybody wants peace and joy and love, goodness and gentleness and faithfulness. Everybody wants to be known as being spiritual, close to God, and walking in the Truth.

So, this is the answer. Every flower and every fruit has a stalk and every stalk has a root, and long before there is any bloom there must be a careful tending of the root and the stalk. This is where the misunderstanding lies—we think that we get the flower and the fragrance and the fruit by some kind of magic, instead of by cultivation.

There is something better than being comfortable

and lazy and relaxed, and Paul is good authority for it: "Be ye therefore followers of God, as dear children; and walk in love, as Christ also hath loved us, and hath given himself for us an offering and a sacrifice to God for a sweetsmelling savour." This is the likeness of Christ in the human heart and life— and our neighbors are waiting to see Him in our lives!

Now, I want to be practical and down-to-earth, and mention a few of the things which I consider to be necessary roots of true Christian living, out of which the fruits and the flowers of deep spirituality appear.

I am thinking first of such necessary spiritual roots as loyalty and faithfulness to God and to His church, the body of Christ on this earth.

Many people boast of their loyalty to their own denomination, but I refer to something greater and more basic than that. I refer to a loyal and prayerful identification with the very cause and truth of Jesus Christ as Lord to the point that we are willing to sacrifice for it. Most Christian churches are already showing signs of a great breakdown in loyalty in these modern times. Every church must have its few who are completely loyal to the implications of Jesus Christ actually being Saviour and Lord and are willing to suffer, if need be, for their love and faith.

Loyalty is surely interwoven with faithfulness, and we do well to remember that Jesus promised His disciples that God would reward us for our faithfulness. In a parable of the kingdom of heaven, Jesus taught that the master, upon his return from the far country, said to his faithful servants, "Well done . . . enter thou into the joy of thy lord."

I know that faithfulness is not a very dramatic subject and there are many among us in the Christian faith who would like to do something with more dash and more flair than just being faithful. Even in our

Christian circles, publicity is considered a great and necessary thing, so we are prone to want to do something that will be recognized, and perhaps get our picture in the paper. Thank God for the loyal and faithful Christians who have only one recognition in mind, and that is 'o hear their Lord say in that Great Day: "Well done . . . enter into the joy of thy Lord."

It is a plain truth that goodness and faithfulness are at the root of much of the consistent fruit-bearing among the witnessing children of God!

In God's Word, the Lord has always placed a great premium on the necessity of faithfulness in those who love Him and serve Him.

Noah was faithful in his day. If old Noah had been a baseball fan or had taken an early retirement or had placed some other interest in his life above God's work, there would have been no ark, no seed preserved and no human race.

Abraham was faithful in his day. If, in his wanderings, Abraham had struck uranium or gold and had given up the idea of going down to Palestine and establishing a people there from whom Jesus Christ would come, what would have happened to God's great plan? If Abraham had turned aside and built himself a little city, making himself mayor and living on the fat of the land, where would we be today?

Moses was faithful in his day. The scriptures leave no doubt about the faithful spirit and ministrations of Moses as God's man for his day and time—"Choosing rather to suffer affliction with the people of God, than to enjoy the pleasures of sin for a season; esteeming the reproach of Christ greater riches than the treasures in Egypt: for he had respect unto the recompence of the reward."

What do we need to say about the faithfulness of our Saviour, Jesus Christ? The world threatened Him all around. The devil was there with his lies and his temptations, offering Jesus the world if He would not go to the cross. But Christ was faithful to His Father and to us. Should we not be faithful to Him? Faithfulness is a wonderful, productive root and out of it comes much fruit.

When we look to our spiritual roots, we dare not dismiss the emphasis of the Word of God on plain, downright honesty and God-ordained goodness in our daily lives.

Honesty that can be trusted and respected is a very fragrant flower in the life of the Christian. Honesty has never yet grown in a vacuum—it is a blossom and a fragrance that grows and develops with spiritual care and nurture. There is a great deal of carelessness about the truth even among Christian believers. Some are surely guilty of stretching the truth about certain things even when they give their Christian testimony. Preachers and evangelists have been known to have exaggerated the numbers and the results of their Christian assemblies.

We joke about such things and forgive the brethren on the basis that their exaggeration was really "evangelistically speaking." But on behalf of God-honoring honesty in our daily lives, it needs to be said that any lie is of its father, the devil, whether it is told in a church service or anywhere else.

God's work does not need pious lies to support it. Rather we ought to follow the spirit of the old saying, "Tell the truth and shame the devil!" In our Christian fellowship, we should be known for being perfectly frank and wholly honest, for honesty has a good root that will also produce other sterling Christian virtues.

Do you know that one of the things that marked the lives of the original Quakers was their honest handling of the truth? They would not lie and they would not stretch the truth. They would not steal and they would not use flattering words. Someone in history wrote about the lives of the Quakers and commented that they "astonished the Christian world

24

by insisting upon acting like Christians." In England they were often kicked around and some languished in jail because they insisted on honoring only God and refused to bow down to people who did not deserve it. In the midst of professing Christians who generally acted like the world, the honest, God-honoring Quakers were considered queer because they sought to live as Christians should.

Many people in our day seem to dream of becoming great while there are far too few who spend any time in concern about being good. The Bible tells us about many good men and few of them would be considered great men. One of them was Jabez, a good man in the Old Testament who is mentioned in only three verses. Saul and Ahab came to places of leadership, and while they were considered great and important men of their times, they were not good men.

The Bible makes it plain to us that our Lord always placed the emphasis upon goodness, rather than upon greatness. Inherently, man does not have a good nature, and that is why Jesus Christ came to this earth and wrought the plan of salvation that makes bad men good. Christ died to wipe away our past sins, to give us new birth, to write our names in the Book of Life, to introduce us to the Father in eternal life.

When we say that Christ died to make us good, we are not being liberal in theology—we are being scriptural. What more can you say about any man than the tribute that he was a good man and full of the Holy Ghost?

Now, let me return to the root of this whole matter—are we Christians willing to be regular in the habits of a holy life, thus learning from the Holy Spirit how to be dependable and faithful, unselfish and Christ-like?

The crops in the fields are regular, and the birds and the animals have a regularity of life. We see it in the rising and the setting of the sun, and in the regularity of the phases of the moon.

The Old Testament revelation itself was built around regularity. It is said of the old man of God that he went into the temple of God in the order of his course and everything in the temple was laid out in order.

God has ordained, as well, that order and regularity may be of immense value to the Christian life.

You should learn to be regular in your prayer life, in your giving to God and His work, and in your church attendance.

But there are too many in the church who say, "I believe in Christ and I have had a spiritual experience and I have the right doctrine"—and then after that go to pieces and become whimsical, and pray according to impulse and give according to the way they feel at the moment, attend church when the weather is good, and do what they do with whimsical irregularity. No wonder they do not carry the sweet fragrance of the Spirit when they come to worship.

It is because people have neglected the root, and the flowers have died. The root of regularity has been forgotten, with the result that when the root is gone, the flowers die shortly thereafter.

But I can hear someone protest, saying, "I wanted to get into the Christian life, the spiritual faith, in order that I might be freed from necessity and from a law of having to do things regularly."

Well, you have missed it, my brother! You might as well close your Bible and walk out because you are in the wrong church and the wrong pew and the wrong dispensation! God would have His people learn regular holy habits and follow them right along day by day.

He doesn't ask us to become slaves to habits, but He does insist that our holy habits of life should become servants of His grace and glory.

Now, of course, this kind of order and regularity in our Christian lives must be tied in with the reality of dependability.

Nature again is the great example of dependability. If you plant corn, you will reap corn. Plant barley and you get barley, not wheat or corn. Set a hen on hens' eggs and you will get chickens, not guinea hens. So with everything after its kind.

Everything is dependable in nature—except man, and even in human society there is a certain amount of dependability.

If your car fails you a few times, you get rid of it, for you need a dependable car. You women know that your refrigerator and freezer must be dependable or the food will spoil unknown to you.

Our monetary system must be dependable, or there would be chaos. What would happen if the dollar was worth a dollar in Chicago, but worth only 75 cents in Milwaukee, 32 cents in St. Louis and in Detroit they wouldn't take it at all?

So, in society we have to know dependability, with the mail and with the milkman and with the schools. You have to be able to trust somebody. The sad thing about it in our human society is that people, as a rule, are trusted and dependable because they get something out of it.

The milkman doesn't come around every morning just because he is a nice fellow; he comes because he is getting paid for it. The mailman doesn't deliver the mail just because he is interested in you and hopes you get a card from Aunt Mabel; he's paid for doing it. The people who make your car build dependability into it because they want you to buy another one, which you won't do if it proves undependable.

How sad to think that it is only at the altar of God that men and women can't be depended upon. Why is it that it is so difficult to find people in the sanctuary who can be depended upon?

The root of dependability is dead in most churches, except for a faithful few, and these few have to take abuse from the unfaithful, undependable ones. The faithful few can always be depended upon and are always in evidence, so they are criticized for wanting to run the show.

Now, I want to ask you a question, and it is not something new and original. Think about your religious life, your holy habits, your church attendance, your giving to the Lord's work, your pattern of dependability during the past 12 months.

Now, be honest with yourselves, and ask an answer of your own heart: "If everyone in this church had been exactly as dependable as I am, where would our church be today?"

That's a question we ought to ask on our knees with tears and with sorrow, praying that God will help us to be dependable. When you are asked to do something, even if it is something simple, do it. It seems that so many of us only want to do the dramatic things—no one wants to be known as being dependable.

If you are waiting until you can do something with a flourish and a flair, something big and grand in the church of God, the chances are that you never will, and if you do, it will simply be a flash in the pan, a rainbow without any meaning, having no final stability!

Why doesn't anyone want to be dependable in the work of Christ?

Brethren, remember that sweet flowers are beautiful to look at and very fragrant to smell, but someone has to be out there on his knees in the dirt, long before there are any blossoms—fertilizing and digging, and going back and doing it again, watching the weather and watering when it gets too dry, and looking after that root.

One of the roots of the Christian life is dependability, and you cannot have spirituality without dependability any more than you can have a begonia without a begonia stalk.

Now, this is probably the place to consider punctuality in the work of God, also.

Isn't it strange that the very fault that would wreck a business, sink a ship, ruin a railroad, is tolerated at the very altar of God?

Why is it that in the church of God so few are concerned about lack of punctuality? The carelessness they show about the work of God would wreck a business or upset the economy, or if done in our bodies would ruin our health.

Now, punctuality is a beautiful thing, but Sunday school teachers don't realize it. Many a Sunday school superintendent has found his hair turning gray because of his worries about getting teachers who will be on time on Sunday morning. Everything we do for God should be done with beautiful precision.

We have a sacred duty. In church and Sunday school, we have in our hands the teaching of immortal souls. We have character to mold and souls to win and the work of God to do.

I have been around a long time and I am convinced that generally people are not spiritual at all if they are not punctual. If they are so lacking in self-discipline and so selfish and so inconsiderate of others and their time that they will not be punctual in the service of God and His church, they are fooling nobody! I repeat it again—if you are not punctual, you are not spiritual!

Everyone can be excused for the emergencies of life—there are accidents that will at times keep any of us from meeting our appointments. But I am trying to show my concern about those who practice the art of not being punctual until it has become a habit in their life.

There isn't anyone important enough to justify that kind of behavior, and anybody that is not punctual, habitually, is guilty of deception and falsehood.

He says he will be there—then he fails to appear!

Punctuality is a beautiful thing. You can't have a rose without a rose bush, and punctuality is the bush on which the rose grows!

So, love and faith, joy and peace may bloom in the heart of the Christian. Beautiful is the Christian character and the sweet smile of the holy man or woman, but that holy life is not by accident nor by coddling. Rather it comes by the bearing of strong burdens, by putting the yoke on his own neck and saying, "For Christ's sake, who bore the cross for me, I will take this self-imposed yoke."

Therefore, let us settle for being good, spiritual people—and let those be great who can! Let us seek first that we might be good, remembering that goodness grows from the roots of obedience, prayer, Bible reading, and surrender. Amen!

Chapter Three

Why Do Men Refuse the Streams of Mercy?

". . . this people refuseth the waters of Shiloah that go softly . . ." Isaiah 8:6

There are, in the Bible, many references where God has used the precious, reviving and life-sustaining qualities of streams of water to give us a true and adequate figure of the gracious, life-giving salvation which He offers all mankind.

He has promised, "I will give you streams of living water."

You will find these scriptural allusions to water and refreshment and cleansing and fruit-bearing in figures of speech, in God's gracious invitations, some spoken in poetic terms.

In the very last chapter of the Bible—in Revelation—God tells us that the Spirit and the bride say "Come," adding that whosoever will may come and "take of the water of life freely."

The historical reference in this text in Isaiah is to the quietly-flowing waters of Shiloah, a stream sometimes wrongly called Siloam.

Shiloah is said to have been the only perennial stream in the city of Jerusalem, the only one that did not dry up seasonally. It seems to me that it is exquisitely named. God Himself must have named it, because this Shiloah means tranquility and rest.

The waters of Shiloah are the waters of tranquility, the peaceful waters that go softly.

The Bible repeats important things often and it is certainly repetitive in making plain that water is one of man's necessary and most valuable assets. It is old and familiar truth that three-fourths of the world's surface is covered with water and that the composition of the human body is 70 per cent water. There is a large water content in our food, as well. Without water there could be no births, no growth, no digestion, no cleansing, no plants, no animals, no atmosphere. Take away water from the face of the earth and this globe we now call our familiar earth would be little more than a parched and ghastly death's head flying endlessly and meaninglessly through space.

But, even above and beyond the scientific interest is the dependence of every farmer and every gardener upon the availability of water.

I recall that when I was a boy I thought the heavy snowfall which covered the fields would smother and freeze the winter wheat and rye, but my father would actually express his thanks, to no one in particular, for the heavy snow cover on the fields. He knew that a good spring crop depended largely upon the heavy snow that kept the ground warm and that the slow melting of the snow in the early spring provided the right kind of moisture.

In some areas of our country, the productivity of the arid land is completely dependent upon the availability of water for irrigation. Farmers everywhere know that they will experience futility and emptiness if there is no water. The crops and fruits and vegetables will never come to fruition without the necessary supply of water. The man tending his herds of animals is in the same situation—for unless he has a place for his cattle to water he cannot use the grazing grounds.

The traveler, too, knows what it would mean to

go into the desert without a supply of water and without a guide. It means to invite death. The simplest way to commit suicide, although not the most painless, would be to walk out across the Sahara or any of the other great deserts of the world without a guide and without sufficient water.

Oh, the precious nature of water—as precious as our blood, of which it is a large part. If there is no water, as in the case of fatal necessity on the desert, there will be a certain and speechless death. This is a strange fact—no one dies crying for water. As he nears death, the poor victim has such swollen tongue and dryness of mouth and cracking of lips that it is impossible to form any words. So, without water, it is not just death but a speechless death—a death that cannot even cry!

When the Lord keeps referring in the scriptures to the precious and necessary streams of living water, He is trying to bring attention and emphasis to the great spiritual needs of the inner man. He is continually hopeful that men and women will heed His truth and admonitions, learning that if streams of water are so vitally important to the well-being and health and welfare of the outer and physical man, how much more should a person be responsive to God's offer of the streams of spiritual life for the immortal part of his being, the soul?

Actually, we find a great preoccupation today with man's physical needs throughout the world. I suppose there never has been a time in the history of the world when there was more interest in the human body than there is today. You can flip open any magazine or periodical and you will find many articles and a great deal of advice about caring for your body, but only occasionally will you find any help for your soul or spirit.

Actually, many people are getting rich, cashing in on our great love for our physical bodies. I must confess that when I read about the many ways in

33

which the human body is groomed and fed and pampered I think about the publicity for Julius the First, a young Angus bull featured in the livestock shows.

You may not believe it, but the owners or handlers of Julius the First brush his teeth every day. They curl the hair on his forehead just like a young fellow brushing himself before he takes off to see his girl. Julius is just an Angus bull, but they brush him and groom him and watch his weight in the hope that he will win the top prizes in the show ring.

What a picture of our humanity! Men and women are brushed and groomed and massaged, intent upon diets and vitamins, completely preoccupied with the outer man, the physical body. The irony of it all is expressed in the fact that in the livestock auction, Julius the First will bring a price of about $16,000— and you know you could not begin to get anything like that for your human body, even in youth, with strength and energy and beauty at their maximum!

Oh, it is the inner man that really matters, for the outward man must perish and go back to the elements from which it was taken, but the inner man lives on and on after the physical body drops away in death.

That body of yours, to which you give so much thought and care, is only the outer tabernacle. The apostle Paul told us about the importance of the inner man and he said he was willing to let the outer man die a little at a time in order that the inner man might be renewed. Throughout the Bible, God emphasizes the value and worth of the inner man, although certainly not to the exclusion of His concern for our physical bodies. We do well to remember the scriptural balance, for the Bible does say that "the Lord is for the body." Certainly, we are putting the emphasis in the wrong place if we become too physical in our outlook, insisting that the most important concern is for the body.

Well, we know for certain that God is much more

concerned with the inner man than with man's outer tabernacle, so He gives us water—the sweet waters, the soft-flowing waters of Shiloah. These are streams of tranquility and peace and He gives them to the inner man.

What a gracious truth—that there is an inner and spiritual man!

Jacob once said, "I go down to Sheol, mourning for my son." Yet, when Jacob died and was buried, they could tell you where his body was. Jacob did not say, "My body will go down." When he said, "I will go down," he was referring to the inner man, that part of him that was the soul, the real Jacob.

On the cross Jesus cried out, "Father, into Thy hands I commit my spirit." They laid His body in the grave and it was there three days, but His inner man, the spirit, was committed unto the Father.

Judas, it is said, went unto his own place—yet we know what happened to his body. It was buried in a field, but Judas himself went unto his own place. There was a Judas, an inner man apart from the body. There was a Jacob apart from the body. There was a Jesus apart from the body.

Abraham's body had been lying in the cave of Machpelah with the dust of centuries upon it when the rich man, Dives, lifted up the eyes of the inner man after his own death and discerned the beggar, Lazarus, resting on Abraham's bosom. It was the real Abraham he discerned—the immortal inner man—there in paradise and it was the real Lazarus who had gone to be with Abraham.

Brothers and sisters, there is a real sense in which we will never know each other until we shuck off this old earthly tabernacle of deception. There is a sense in which our bodies actually veil us from one another. We are uncertain. We shake a hand and look at a face. The influence of that hand or face is a physical thing—and the real you, the inner man, is deeper than that, and beyond and past all of that.

What did it actually mean for mankind when Jesus Christ came into our world?

No one should think for even one second that He came just to bring a state of peace between nations, or that He came merely to give prosperity so we would all have richer food to eat, softer beds in which to sleep and finer homes in which to live!

God's Word leaves no doubt about it—Jesus came in order that our spirits might prosper! He came that our inner man, the eternal and undying part of us, might prosper! He died to open a fountain of such gracious nature that to partake and drink means a spiritual transformation, never to hunger and thirst again for temporal and passing things.

Now, what is this water, this softly-flowing stream of peace and tranquility and rest? God wants us to be sure—either we know or we do not know!

If this is not a reality, it is simply poetry with which I am regaling you to earn my living.

I ask you: can you not put aside all of the poetry and figure and metaphor and get through to something basic and solid and real, where you can say, "Thank God there is mercy and forgiveness and cleansing and eternal life for the guilty soul, the inner man who has sinned!"?

I heard the voice of Jesus say,
Behold, I freely give
The living waters; thirsty one
Stoop down and drink and live!

I came to Jesus, and I drank
Of that life-giving stream,
My thirst was quenched, my soul revived,
And now I live in Him!

There it is—there is the mercy of God! Man's great difficulty is that we have religion without guilt, and religion without guilt just tries to make God a big "pal" of man. But religion without guilt is a religion that cannot escape hell for it deceives and finally destroys all who are a part of it.

Religion without any consciousness of guilt is a false religion. If I come to Jesus Christ without any confession of guilt, simply to gain some benefit, I still have woe upon me, as did the Pharisees before me! But if my guilt drives me to Jesus, then I have my guilt taken from me and I find mercy. Oh, the mercy of God! We sing about the mercy of God, and I hope we know what we are singing about: "O depths of mercy, can it be, that gate is left ajar for me."

The good mercy of God—that is the water to a thirsty man—the man whose conscious guilt and sin are causing him pain and anguish.

That thirsty man can come to the Lord Jesus and drink of the waters of Shiloah—the waters of mercy!

My brother, you will never have inward peace until you have acknowledged your guilt. This is something you cannot dodge and evade, because you have a conscience and your conscience will never let you rest until you get rid of the guilt!

Guilt must be dealt with and taken away! Oh, you can be smoothed over and given a little theological massage, patted on the head and told that it is all right, but that treatment will not take away guilt and condemnation. Sins that you thought were absolved by religion will always come back to haunt you.

Only the Redeemer and Saviour, Jesus Christ, can forgive and pardon and free from guilt—and the sins He has forgiven will never come back to haunt you as a child of God—never while the world stands! He forgives and forgets, burying your old load of guilt so that it no longer exists. God has promised, "I will not remember thy guilt." Since God is able to remember everything, the only way to figure this is that God beats that guilt and condemnation back out of being so it does not even exist any more! The sin that God pardons is no longer an entity—it is gone forever!

Christians have often talked about the "covering" of our sins and I know it is a common phrase. I have used it myself, but it is a figure of speech—for sin is not covered. The sinner must be cleansed. Let me explain. In the Old Testament, sin was covered as they waited for the Lamb to come and die on the cross! But in the New Testament sinners could look back on the finished work already done by Christ, blood already spilled. Sins are not covered now. They are cleansed and forgiven! That is why the believing Christian can have inward peace and joy.

There it is—the water of grace, the flow of mercy to the sinner, poverty stricken and spiritually bankrupt. The grace of our Lord Jesus Christ flows like the waters of Shiloah—the quiet waters that are so readily available.

Did you know that sheep cannot drink from noisy, running water? A sheep's nostrils are so close to his mouth that if he starts to drink and the water is moving, he will choke and could perhaps drown. It is necessary for the shepherd to dam the stream until a quiet pool is formed, and the moving water becomes still. Then the animal can put his muzzle into the water and drink without choking and gasping for air. When David wrote about our Lord being our shepherd, he said, "He leadeth me beside the still water."

The grace of God is like the still, quiet pool of water. The water flows softly! Oh, Grace of God, how you have been wounded in the house of your friends! Grace of God, how you have been made into a fetish before which modern men bow in worship. The sweet grace of God—how it has been used to hide what people really are. The grace of God has been preached in ways that have damned men instead of saved them. Yet it is still full and free—the grace of God!

If God could not extend us His mercy and grace, and treated us exactly as we deserved, there would be only one course for Him to follow. God would have to turn an angered face to us in life and He would have to turn His back to us in death. That would happen to the best human beings that ever lived, if we should receive only what we deserve.

But, oh, the grace of God! God through the plan of salvation in Jesus Christ will go beyond our merits, beyond that which we deserve. Even if our sins have been like a mountain, it is the grace of God that assures our forgiveness. There is cleansing for the defiled, gracious and satisfying cleansing—a beautiful element in Christianity as revealed by the Lord Himself, and not just abstract theology.

I saw a magazine cover which pictured four men. It was an unusual picture for it showed the youngest man preaching his first sermon, for he had just come out of prison where he had received Christ—a redeemed, converted, transformed follower of Jesus, now determined to tell others the good news. With him was the pastor of the church in which the young man was preaching, the lawyer who had been the prosecutor in his trial, and the judge who had sentenced him to prison. Many judges and lawyers will admit that when most criminals are returned to a happy and useful life it is because they have purgation in the blood of the Lamb, the power of Christ to change a man, to cleanse from defilement, to transform his life and character.

This is a beautiful thing—that a former car thief can stand with a big grin on his face and hold an open Bible in his hand, and witness to the power of the Christian gospel.

Men will ask: How can it be? Because the blood of Jesus Christ cleanses from all sin. Because there is a fiery purgation in the Christian message that can take any sinful man and make him clean and make him good, for Christ's sake!

Knowing the power of this gospel, I am willing to put myself on record that I would rather be preached to by a converted car thief than be lulled to death by the educated gentlemen who have reduced Christianity to nothing more than a psychology of comfort. Even their church ads woo men and women with the appeal, "Come to church and be comforted."

Brothers and sisters in Christ's church, you do not want consolation and comfort—you want to know the facts, you want to know where you stand before God Almighty!

In recent days I have had two persons come to me personally to tell me that my preaching has been cutting them to pieces, making them miserable and desirous of something better God has for them in their lives.

I think that is a beautiful thing and I thank God that I am worthy of that. People should not come to Christ and to His church with the expectation that all spiritual problems are consummated in comfort and consolation. If that is all people want in their church going, they will find a large number of preachers waiting to rock them to sleep with the consolation, "Bye, bye now, and here's your bottle!"

What do we know about today? Any of us can have a sudden heart attack and be called from this life. How will it be with our souls and where will we go—those are the things we want to know for sure. Following Christ, we want to know how we can go on to be holy and live holy and be right with God, turning our backs on sin and living in the Spirit!

Men are always faced with choices and decisions as the loving and eternal God deals with them, now in mercy and in patience.

I must confess as a pastor and minister that I

have had to say "Goodbye" to people in some instances when they have said: "We cannot worship here. You are too strict. Your standards are too strict for this day and age. Your message is too strict!"

My only apology is that I am still not as strict as the Bible is. I have to confess that I am still not up to the standard of the scriptures. I am trying, but I am not that strict.

But, occasionally, we have to say farewell to someone who says they have to find a different kind of church, an easy-going church, a church that majors in relaxation.

What did Jesus say to us? He said that unless we are ready to turn from everything and follow Him with devotion, we are not yet ready to be His disciples, and unless we are ready to die for Him, we are not ready to live for Him. The whistle is going to blow for us one of these days and then we will have to appear and tell God how we carried on His work, how we conducted ourselves in the light of what Jesus said.

So we cannot afford to let down our Christian standards just to hold the interest of people who want to go to hell and still belong to a church. We have had carnal and fleshly and self-loving people who wanted to come in and control young people's groups and liberate us from our spiritual life and standards and "strictness."

I would like to know why people of that kind of disposition want to go to church. I know what I would do if I were determined just to eat, drink and be merry—I would never want to show up among people who are devoted to Jesus Christ and to His saving gospel. If I were of that mind and disposition and found myself at church, I would at least go to the furnace room and stay there until church was over!

I thank God for Christian men and women who want to know the facts and the truth as it has come from God. Thank God, they are not just looking for someone to give them a relaxing religious massage! These are the facts—the blood of Jesus Christ cleanses. There is a purging element in Christianity. Then there is the Holy Spirit, the blessed Spirit of God who brings us the peace and tranquility of the waters of Shiloah.

The living God invites us to this stream, the only perennial stream in the world, the only stream that never runs dry, the only stream that never overflows and destroys.

Yet, the prophet Isaiah went on to record the fact that he could not understand how the people of Israel could refuse the soft-flowing waters sent by the Lord.

The prophet voiced his incredulity and amazement: "How can it be? Israel refuses the soft waters of Shiloah sent by the Lord; the healing, tranquilizing stream that brings peace to the heart and conscience. They refuse it and turn to men like themselves instead."

Isaiah then warned that those who refuse the still and peaceful streams from God have only one thing to anticipate—the overflowing torrents of judgment. He said, "If ye choose to turn away from the soft waters of Shiloah, the Lord God bringeth upon you the waters of the river, strong and many, and he shall come over all his channels, and go over all his banks."

I do not think we are overly-serious in our approach. I do not think we have made extreme statements, statements that need modification, in light of New Testament truth given by our Lord Jesus Christ. I do not think we are as severe as God would have us be in the facing of coming judgment, for it was Jesus Himself who told the Jews in His day, "The Father . . . hath committed all judgment unto the Son."

Chapter Four

How Can a Moral Man
Ever Find Saving Truth?

*"Jesus said unto him, If thou wilt be perfect, go
and sell that thou hast, and give to the poor, and
thou shalt have treasure in heaven: and come and
follow me.*
*"But when the young man heard that saying, he
went away sorrowful: for he had great possessions."*
Matthew 19:21-22

I have never felt that it was my ministry to personally expose or defrock those whose religious views
happen to fall far short of the New Testament demands of Jesus Christ, but I do believe there is one
man in the New Testament record whose "debunk-
ing" has been delayed almost 2,000 years.

I refer, of course, to that person who has become
so well known to Bible students and to Christian
audiences as "the rich young ruler" who came to
Jesus to talk about the terms of eternal life.

Christian congregations throughout the years
have heard a countless number of sermons in which
this young religious leader has been portrayed as
a Sir Galahad of his time—"whose strength was as
the strength of ten because his heart was pure."

Personally, I have found it strangely amazing to
look back into the records of scholars and preachers

and find that great ranks of religious people down the years have misunderstood the manner in which Jesus dealt with this inquirer.

Almost everyone has gone over to the side of this young man in accepting his word as valid testimony when he said: "The commandments? All of these I have kept from my youth up!"

"I have kept them," he said. So there is a great chorus of moral applause and for centuries that nameless man has been preached and praised as a paragon of morality and a sincere seeker after truth.

There are several things for us to review as we consider this incident in the earthly life of our Lord. Perhaps the most common misunderstanding about the "rich young ruler" is the presumption of many that he was a political or government leader, but the gospel records indicate that he was a religious leader among the Jews, probably in one of the synagogues. The word *ruler* should not indicate to us a man with crown and scepter and a robe—it simply means that the man was a chairman, a president, a leader of a local worshipping group.

Another thing to notice is that even though he was recognized among those in religious circles, he was still trying to satisfy the uncertainties of his own inner life. I mention this because it makes it appear that things have not changed a great deal in 2,000 years. Personally, I have never before had a year in which so many persons of high place and status in church circles have sought me out for counsel regarding their own spiritual condition and problems. The point I make is this: these are not beginners in the faith. They are not unbelievers. Some are highly placed in our own evangelical circles.

What can be wrong when religious leaders are uncertain and shaken and miserable? I say that they have been brought into the Christian faith without any confrontation with total commitment to Jesus Christ as Lord, without any instruction that Christian victory means complete abandonment of our self and person to Jesus Christ!

Now, this review of the gospel record: This young Jewish leader came to Jesus, asking, "Good master, what good thing shall I do, that I may have eternal life?"

Jesus answered, "Why do you call me good? There is only one who is truly good and that is God; but if you will enter into life, keep the commandments."

Then, looking into Jesus' face, he asked: "Which commandments? Are you teaching some commandments that I do not know about?"

The answer Jesus gave him was direct: "No, I am talking about the regular commandments with which you are familiar as a religious Jew. God's commands: Thou shalt do no murder, thou shalt not commit adultery—you know them all."

It was then that the young man, looking into the face of Jesus Christ, said: "All of these things I have kept from my youth—what lack I yet?"

Jesus then gave him the opportunity for spiritual decision—the opportunity of self-renunciation, the privilege of putting spiritual things above material things, the complete abandonment of himself as a follower and disciple of Jesus, God's Son, and messianic provision for lost men.

There follows one of the sad and depressing statements of the New Testament record: "But when the young man heard that saying, he went away sorrowful, for he had great possessions."

Let us notice a great truth here—a religious life and religious practice have never provided the eternal assurance for which the heart longs. This young man was in religious leadership and yet he came to Jesus to discuss the void in his own being. He wanted something more than a conclusion drawn from a text. He was undoubtedly groping for the knowledge in his own heart that he had entered into a state of eternal benediction—we refer to it now as the assurance of eternal life.

His question to Jesus was: "What good thing must I do?"

Remember that our Lord Jesus Christ had never studied the books, but He was a master in dealing with people. He was a master psychologist, which means simply that He knew the ways of men and how their minds work. That is the basis of true psychology, anyway.

Jesus heard what this young man said and immediately was able to appraise him. Jesus knew that he was a religious leader. Jesus knew that he read the Hebrew scriptures and that he lifted his hands to God and led the people in their ancient prayers. Yet Jesus knew that he was not satisfied, that he was still miserable because of the aching lack within his own being.

In dealing with him, Jesus took him where he found him, and for the sake of the argument, He accepted him at his own estimate.

"You have come to talk to me, and you lay this matter of your relationship to God and eternal life on the foundation of doing good things to obtain life," Jesus reminded him.

"Just how good would that good thing have to be?" Jesus continued. "You do know there is only one good and that is God, and if you are going to do something good enough to move God to give you the gift of eternal life, how good must your action be?

"Seeing there is only one good, and you do not believe I am God, for you called me good master and good teacher, all in the same breath, what could you do that would be good enough? How are you going to be good enough if there is only one good and that is God? To win anything from God on the devil's terms, you would have to do something good enough for God to accept.

"So, young man, if you insist on buying your way in, I have the answer: Keep the commandments. That is the way you will have to do it."

The reply to Jesus was, "All of these I have kept from my youth up."

Now, we will all agree that without doubt this young man had kept certain of the commandments from his youth. I doubt that he had ever murdered anyone. He had probably never committed adultery. I suppose it had never been necessary for him to steal. Probably he had honored his father and mother, for the Jews did this, as a rule.

This young man has been praised so often in sermons because he was what we call "a moral man." Let me tell you what a moral man really is: he is good enough to deceive himself and bad enough to damn himself!

This young man did not realize the danger of being a moral man. He was self-deceived—and because his goodness prevented him from knowing his badness, he turned his back on God and walked away.

It is plain in every age that many men and women deceive themselves by accepting the idea that any kind of religion is all right, any kind of religion will do.

Is any kind of old mustard plaster all right in dealing with cancer in the body?

Is any kind of food all right for the health and growth of a tiny baby?

Is any kind of old beat-up airplane all right for transporting men and women through the skies, several miles above the earth?

No, my friends. Sometimes, having anything is worse than having nothing. Frankly, I would much rather have no religion at all than to have just enough to deceive me.

This was the downfall of this rich young ruler.

He had just enough religion to delude himself and deceive himself. He was just good enough to make himself think that he was all right, to answer that he had kept God's laws.

I am going to ask you to decide whether he had—or not.

The Bible says, "Thou shalt have no other gods before me."

I believe that Jew and Catholic and Protestant all would agree that whatever comes before God is god to them, and that whatever shuts out God and stands between the soul and God is an idol, a god.

This young man knew very well the command that God must have first place in our lives. Yet, he was very rich and when our Lord put to him on his own terms the question of selling everything and giving it away, making God first in his life and becoming a disciple, he turned his back on it.

He turned his back on God because he had another god that he loved, although he would not admit it. He was able to lead the people in worship and in prayer and in the songs of Zion, but unknown to them, he had a god, an idol, tucked away. When the chips were down, he chose the god of gold instead of the God of his fathers.

I say that the rich young ruler was not a keeper of the law. He shattered and smashed the first one like a glass on the pavement. When the God of his fathers instructed, "Sell everything and follow me," he turned his back and walked away.

Again, our Lord summed up all of the commandments in His words: "Thou shalt love the Lord thy God with all thy heart."

When this young man came face to face with the vital question of his love for God or his love of wealth, he went away because he had great possessions. So, he broke and shattered this summation of all of the commandments of God.

Jesus also coupled with love of God the command

48

that "thou shalt love thy neighbor as thyself."

Even as this young man talked with Jesus, the poor and the beggars and the crippled and the starving were all around them. Old men and women in poverty, little children without enough food to eat, lepers trying to find roots and grasshoppers and snails in an effort to keep their emaciated and ailing bodies from falling apart.

Yet, knowing the reality of human need for countless thousands, this young man could stand in the temple and pray and lead out in song in an effort to glorify his God and Abraham, Isaac and Jacob. When Jesus suggested that, as a condition of following Him, he distribute his earthly goods, the young man flatly refused.

Surely, he did not exactly love his neighbor as himself. But in his own eyes he was a noble keeper of the law. He could stand and say to Jesus, "All of these I have kept." I do not believe he was lying—but he was terribly deceived.

The last commandment in the decalogue says to every man: "Thou shalt not covet."

This means a great many things, for the word *covet* in the rest of the Bible, in both the Old and New Testaments, clearly means wanting anything with inordinate desire.

The young man shattered that one wide open, even as Jesus talked with him: "Distribute thy goods, and come and follow me—like Peter and the rest. We may be known as poor, but we owe nothing. I owe nothing. Come and go with me—for there is a regeneration taking place."

But he refused. He was unable to leave his bank accounts and his properties. So, he was a covetous man. He was a lover of self instead of loving his neighbor. He was a lover of his own wealth rather than loving God with his innermost being. The living God was not first in his life and in his love—and so the commandments were broken.

There is an important teaching for each of us here.

It is entirely possible for us to imagine ourselves to be all right when we are not all right. It is entirely possible to jockey our souls around over the checkerboard of our conscience to make everything appear to be all right.

That's what this moral young man was doing as Jesus talked to him and instructed him. It is well to note that our Lord plainly faced him with the terms of eternal salvation: full acknowledgement of sin rather than a defensive attitude, complete trust in the person of Jesus Christ, and utter abandonment to His Lordship alone.

Actually, there have never been any other terms laid down for salvation anywhere or at any time. Men with their multitudes of petty gods are still like this young man—ready to declare their own goodness even while standing knee-deep in broken laws.

A man who truly comes to God in repentance and contrition of heart does not work up a defense on the basis that he has not broken every law and every commandment. If he is truly penitent in seeking pardon and forgiveness, he will be so overcome with the guilt of the commands that he has broken and the sins he is confessing that he will be down before the great God Almighty, trembling and crying out, "Oh, God, I am an unclean man and I have sinned against Thee!"

Remember, an outlaw is not a man who has broken all the laws of his country—he may actually have ignored and flouted and violated only a few. The bandit Jessie James may have broken only a couple of laws—those that say "You shall not kill" and "You shall not steal." But he was a notorious outlaw with a price on his head, even though there were thousands of other laws on the books which he had not violated.

Brethren, when I come before my God as an outlaw, returning home as the prodigal, returning from the pig pen, I will not be dickering and bargaining with God about the sins that I did not commit. I will not even be conscious of those—for the fact that I have broken any of God's laws or committed any sins will so overwhelm me that I will go before God as though I were the worst sinner in all the wide world.

The defensive attitude of "moral" men and women is one of the great problems confronting Christianity in our day. Many who are trying to be Christians are making the effort on the basis that they have not done some of the evil things which others have done. They are not willing to honestly look into their own hearts, for if they did, they would cry out in conviction for being the chief of all sinners.

Look at the record of the apostle Paul. He took an honest look at his own sinful nature, and the fact that he had committed any sin at all bit down so hard on him that it crushed him like an eggshell.

Paul could testify that as far as conscience was concerned, he had tried to honor it. As far as was humanly possible, as a member of one of the strictest sects, he had been concerned with keeping the laws of God. Actually, no one can go into the record and try to pin the awful, daily variety of gross and heinous sins on Paul, for, in most ways, he was a strong and noble and moral man. He did the best he could in his own unregenerate state before he met Jesus Christ. But out of his own crushed heart, after experiencing the transformation that Christ brings within, Paul confessed that he saw his own being as God had seen it: "I am chief of sinners. I have been the worst sinner in the world!"

Oh, the difference Jesus Christ makes in our attitudes!

Because Paul finally saw himself as the worst man in the world, God could make him one of the best men in the world and in history.

The rich young ruler never had this sense of his

own sin and unworthiness. He dared to stand before Jesus Christ, of whom he was inquiring the way of eternal life, and defend himself.

"I am no heathen," he said. "I have kept God's laws."

Oh, how wrong he was. The very fact that he could remember that he had kept any of God's laws disqualified him instantly for eternal life. He trusted in his own moral defense rather than acknowledge his sin and his need.

Now, the matter of complete trust in the person of Christ.

No man has any hope for eternal salvation apart from trusting completely in Jesus Christ and His atonement for men. Simply stated, our Lord Jesus is the lifeboat and we must fully and truly be committed to trusting the lifeboat.

Again, our Lord and Saviour is the rope by which it is possible to escape from the burning building. There is no doubt about it—either we trust that rope or we perish.

He is the wonder drug or medication that heals all ills and sicknesses—and if we refuse it, we die.

He is the bridge from hell to heaven—and we take the bridge and cross over by His grace or we stay in hell.

These are simple illustrations, but they get to the point of the necessity of complete trust in Jesus Christ—absolute trust in Him!

I wonder how many people in our own day really trust Christ in that way. There are so many who want to trust Christ plus something else. They want to trust Christ and add their own morals. They want to trust Christ and add their own good works. They want to trust Christ and then point to the merits of their baptism or church membership or stewardship.

Let me tell you straight out that Jesus Christ will never stand at the right side of a plus sign. If you will insist upon adding some "plus" to your faith in Jesus Christ, He will walk away in His holy dignity. He will ever refuse to be considered the other part of a "plus" sign. If your trust is in the plus—something added—then you do not possess Jesus Christ at all.

The rich young ruler thought that he possessed all of the necessary plus signs. The truth was that he possessed nothing that really mattered.

Then, a man's salvation involves utter abandonment to Jesus Christ. Our Lord taught this fundamental truth throughout His earthly ministry, so it was not a new concept proposed for the rich young ruler. Jesus skillfully got that man into a place where He could clearly and plainly tell him this great fact of the spiritual life: "Do not keep anything in your life that is more important than God Himself; come and follow me in complete trust and abandonment!"

I wonder also how many Christians in our day have truly and completely abandoned themselves to Jesus Christ as their Lord. We are very busy telling people to "*accept* Christ"—and that seems to be the only word we are using. We arrange a painless acceptance.

We are telling people that the easiest thing in the world is to *accept* Jesus Christ, and I wonder what has happened to our Christian theology which no longer contains any hint of what it should mean to be completely and utterly abandoned to Jesus Christ, our Lord and Saviour.

I think it is a good sign that we are having a restlessness and a dissatisfaction among professing Christians concerning their own spiritual state. I find that we are having to start all over with many of them because they have never been taught anything but "the acceptance of Christ." They need the plain statement of the terms of eternal salvation: acknowledgement of sin and complete trust in Christ and utter abandonment to Him and His Lordship.

At this point, the rich young ruler was not interested. These were terms that he had not anticipated and he could not accept them at all. So, we read in the scripture: "He, sorrowing, went away."

You see, like all men, he had a basic interest in eternal life, but there were other things that he wanted more! No doubt he had some urge to follow Christ as the Messiah, but there were other things he wanted more!

Let me point out here something I feel about this young man and many others like him who live around us today.

I do not believe that every person who is spiritually unbelieving and lost is morally careless. We all know men and women who care very deeply about life, about evil conditions and changing moral standards. Many of them work and teach and try to do the best they can—but they are still lost because they have never acknowledged God's terms for eternal salvation and they are not abandoned to Jesus Christ, our Lord.

It is not only the careless who perish. Those who are careful and busy about many good things will perish as well. The rich young ruler took the human way and perished, even though he cared enough to come to Jesus and ask the way of life in a reverent and tender question.

He was a religious man of his day—but he was a lost man. He was a sinner, a law-breaker, a rebel—and the Lord quickly brought the truth to the surface.

It is actually true that many people engage in earnest prayers on their road to perdition. In a way, they want God, but they don't want Him enough. They are interested in eternal life, but they are still more interested in other things. They know that they should follow Jesus in true faith, but other things keep them from that decision.

I hope that God can burn this frightful fact into our souls—the truth that men and women can be respectable and religious and prayerful and careful and eager and ask the right questions and talk about religion—and still be lost!

In our churches today, we feel that we have found a real treasure if we find someone who appears to be eagerly seeking the truth of God. Actually, we rarely find anyone who seems to be as eager as the rich young man who came to Jesus.

They don't seem to be coming to us in the churches. We have to go out after them—joke with them, talk with them about their sports, try to find some common ground, and then gingerly tell them that if they will receive Jesus they will have peace of mind, good grades in school and everything will be all right. Amen!

Now, that is a fair run-down on modern Christianity, and it explains why there are Christians who ask, "What's the matter with me, brother? What's the matter with me?"

They have not come into the kingdom of God through repentance and trust and abandonment. The result is exactly what we would expect in those who have been "leaked" into the kingdom of God, taken in between the cracks, crawling in through a side window. There is no inner witness. There is no assurance. There is no inward peace.

When we think we have found someone who is a seeker, we settle back and say, "That's wonderful! He will be all right—he is a seeker."

Here is the caution, brethren: if you could see all the seekers who are in hell today who were seekers while they were on earth, you would know that many have sought and found out what they had to do—and then refused to do it.

This rich young ruler was a seeker. The church today would have put his name down on a card and would have counted him among the statistics. But he walked away and turned his back on the offer and the appeal of Jesus Christ.

Every faithful pastor can tell you, with great sorrow and concern, the stories of young people and men and women who walked away from the church and straight Bible teaching and warm Christian fellowship to have their own way. When the old nature stirred, they turned their backs on God and walked away. They went into questionable marriages. They went into worldly alliances. They took jobs in which there was no chance to please and glorify God. They went back into the world.

Now, they did not walk out of the house of God because they did not want God—but because they found something they wanted more than God! God has given men and women the opportunity for free will and free choices—and some are determined to have what they want most.

The rich young ruler made his decision on the basis of what he wanted most in life. The last thing we know about him is the fact that he turned from Jesus and walked away. He was sorry about it and sorrowful, because he had great earthly possessions. But Jesus looked upon him as he walked away and Jesus was sorrowful, too.

Those who walk away from Christian fellowship, leaving the church and the choir, directly into the arms of sinners, do not actually leave with happiness and great joy. I have had some of them who came back to counsel and consult with me. I believe they are trying to get a pastoral excuse or rationalization for the manner in which they turned their backs on God.

I have committed sins in my day which I believe the blood of the everlasting covenant has cleansed and blotted away forever—but that kind of rationalization is not one of them. I can say that I have never told anyone, "It will be all right; don't worry about it," when it was not all right, in fact. There are many virtues as a minister that I do not have, but those who have turned their backs on God and wanted me to give them some excuse have found that they have never succeeded in softening me up.

People often come to me to find out where they have missed the secret of the victorious and joyful Christian life. Generally, I discover that they want to live in two worlds. They want to live a holy life like Dr. A. B. Simpson, but at the same time they want to be as worldly as the heathen. They aspire to the saintliness of the saintly McCheyne, but they are satisfied to be as worldly as the world—and it is impossible to have both!

I admit that there are parents who counsel me about the danger of losing the young people from our church life because I am faithful in preaching against this present world and the worldly system in which we live.

I can only say that I am concerned and I will stand and cry at the door when they decide to go, but I will not be guilty of deceiving them. I refuse to deceive and damn them by teaching that you can be a Christian and love this present world, for you cannot.

Yes, you can be a hypocrite and love the world.

You can be a deceived ruler in the religious system and love the world.

You can be a cheap, snobbish, modern Christian and love the world.

But you cannot be a genuine Bible Christian and love the world. It would grieve me to stand alone on this principle, but I will not lie to you about it.

The rich young ruler wanted God, but he turned back to his money and possessions. He was grieved within himself that he had to pay such a price— the true knowledge of eternal life—in order to keep the things he loved the most.

How about the men and women all around us who seem satisfied with their choice of this present world, having turned their backs on God? They are determined to have and to hold what they love the most, but they are actually grieved at the knowledge of what it has cost them to have their own way. They choose and take what they want, but they grieve for the God they have deserted.

We have many like the rich young ruler among us still. It is not enough to inquire about the power of the crucified life and the Spirit-filled life. It is not enough to want it—it must be desired and claimed above everything else. There must be an abandonment to Jesus Christ to realize it. The individual must want the fullness of Christ with such desire that he will turn his back on whatever else matters in his life and walk straight to the arms of Jesus!

So much for the case of the rich young ruler. His veil was taken away and he turned from Jesus Christ. He was still the hypocrite, still a covetous man, a money-lover, a breaker of the law. Above all, he was still a sinner, and Christless.

He had to pay a great price to keep what he loved most. Actually, he had to sell Jesus even as Judas Iscariot sold Him. Judas sold Him for 30 pieces of silver. We have no idea in terms of money and land and possessions what the rich young ruler paid in his refusal to follow Jesus.

I do not think I have been over-serious in this appraisal of what it means to become a true and devoted disciple of Jesus Christ. I do not think I have been as severe as the New Testament actually tells it. And I do not think I have said as much as Jesus said when He laid down His terms of discipleship in the New Testament.

What about you? If you are a seeker after Jesus Christ in truth, He is saying to you: "It is not enough to inquire. Give up that which is the dearest thing you hold in life; and come, and follow me!"

Chapter Five

What Is It Costing You to Be a Christian?

"And then shall appear the sign of the Son of man in heaven: and then shall all the tribes of the earth mourn, and they shall see the Son of man coming in the clouds of heaven with power and great glory."
Matthew 24:30

It is very easy in our day to discern a glaring inconsistency among many well-groomed and overfed evangelical Christians, who profess that they are looking for Christ's second coming and yet vigorously reject any suggestion that Christian faith and witness should be costing them something.

I have come to believe that when we discuss the prophetic scriptures and the promises of the Lord Jesus Christ that He will return, we must necessarily examine the kind of love we really have for Him in our hearts.

If we are soon going to look upon His blessed face, should we not be expecting that He will search out the true nature of the love and adoration which we profess?

The Bible makes it plain that the love of many shall wax cold in the terrible and trying period just before Jesus does return to earth. It is well, then, to face up to a searching question:

"How ardent, how genuine, and how meaningful is your love for the Lord Jesus Christ?"

A second question follows in quick succession: "What are you doing to prove your love for the Saviour? What is your faith and witness of Jesus Christ actually costing you in your daily life?"

I confess that a preacher cannot bring this kind of message to laymen without making a request for prayer on his own behalf. I do believe that we are living in those times that Jesus said would come when the love and concern of many would wax cold.

Will you pray for me as a minister of the gospel? I am not asking you to pray for the things people commonly pray for. Pray for me in light of the pressures of our times. Pray that I will not just come to a wearied end—an exhausted, tired, old preacher, interested only in hunting a place to roost. Pray that I will be willing to let my Christian experience and Christian standards cost me something right down to the last gasp!

It is impossible for us to dismiss the explicit teachings of our Lord Jesus concerning the end of this age and His return to earth. It is impossible to dismiss the emphasis of the entire Bible concerning God's plan for this earth and the consummation of all things. A large percentage of Bible truth is actually predictive in nature, telling us what will come to pass. Some of these passages are already fulfilled. Others remain to be fulfilled.

When the World Council of Churches held one of its most important international assemblies in Evanston, we were struck by the unusual significance of the theme, "Christ, the Hope of the World."

It turned out that many of the American and European leaders of the World Council were embarrassed when many of the representatives of overseas Christian groups interpreted the theme to mean that the hope of the world lies in the second return of Christ to our earth.

Actually, the leaders were embarrassed because they had been playing down any emphasis upon the prophetic scriptures for years, and because they denied all reality in relationship to a visible and specific return of Jesus Christ to this earth.

I can think of at least three reasons why the strenuous effort was made to contain the discussions and to keep the world delegations from coming out with a clear-cut statement on the second coming of Christ as the world's greatest hope.

First, there are many churchmen and church organizations which have their own ideas for society and for their own nations. Bible prophecy concerning the return of Christ does not fit in with those ideas at all.

Second, these men and their groups are well aware of the spiritual implications of Christ's prophecies, and to believe sincerely in His return would necessitate a willing separation from this world system and its ungodly practices.

Third is the immediate rejection of any kind of link with literal Bible prophecy because of those who have made themselves ridiculous by insisting upon their own wild speculations and by going far beyond the bounds of interpretation set in the scriptures themselves.

Some basic things should be very clear to all. Our Lord taught that He would come back to earth again. The chosen apostles taught that the Saviour would come back to earth to reign. For centuries the church fathers emphasized that Jesus would return to earth as the final and ultimate hope and consolation of the Christian church.

At the time of the ascension of Christ, the angelic message assured that "this same Jesus, which is taken up from you into heaven, shall so come in like manner as ye have seen him go into heaven."

Most of us have encountered the glib explanations

of those who refuse any literal interpretation of the prophetic words.

Through the years, some have taught that the return of Christ was fulfilled in the destruction of Jerusalem. That is so ridiculous that I see no reason for attempting to refute it.

Others have been satisfied to believe that Christ's promise of returning to the earth has been fulfilled over and over again when Christians die. However, the scriptures plainly teach that in God's great plan for humans and for this earth, there would be only two advents—one, to die; and the other, to reign. If Christ were keeping His promise to return to earth every time a Christian dies, it would leave no basis for the clear instructions He gave concerning two climactic and significant advents to earth.

Well, it is evident that no one can study the implications of the prophetic scriptures without realizing that in our generation we are living in days which are not only grave and sobering, but are grand days, as well.

Grave and grand—dramatic days! Greater days than you and I realize. Solemn days in which we are to give heed to the prophetic scriptures.

Now, I do not say that any of us can stand and proclaim and predict the world developments as if by schedule. The Bible does not have a schedule like the local train—giving the name of every stop and the time it will arrive and the time it will leave.

For anyone to say that the scriptures can be interpreted in that way is to distort and misinterpret prophetic truth. The Bible is a book of great and grand outlook and scope, and it tells us of the future, but it tells us in great, sweeping strokes like an artist painting a picture across the sky. The size would be so tremendous that you would have to retreat to a point far away to sense it and take it in. There would be no place in that kind of painting for tiny details, with vast brush strokes that would start with one star and extend across to another.

So, we cannot predict for one another what may come tomorrow. Not even the angels know that—our tomorrow is in the knowledge only of our Father in heaven.

It is not only the little fellow, the common man, who is helpless to predict how things may fall in the future—the great leaders in world society are just as helpless.

Leaders and groups and nations often think they have something great and enduring and superior going for them in human society, and because we don't jump on the bandwagon and remark, instead, that "This, too, will pass away," we get a look of anger with the comment, "You are a cynical pessimist."

Let me say that it is very difficult to have any brains in this day in which we live and not get blamed for it. It is hard to have any insight and not be considered a cynic. It is hard to be realistic and not be classed with the pessimists.

But with most men and their methods and movements in society, a few months, at the most a few years, bring an entirely new perspective. People who disagreed with you and were engaged in flag-waving for someone's scheme or speech six months ago are probably looking back on that same thing and see it now just as you foresaw it.

It is a wonderfully exhilarating thing to be able to anticipate and foresee just a little bit—but it is also an ability that will bring you much criticism and hostility from those with lesser foresight and judgment.

Well, the great men of the earth are still only men. Think what they would be willing to give for a supernatural gift of foretelling events of the future! The world leaders must be great men in some respects; otherwise, we would be there and they would be here!

But, if I am not mistaken, it will be the great

men of the earth who will be crying for the mountains to fall on them in the coming day of judgment, according to the book of Revelation.

Again, if I am not mistaken, there was not one man considered great in human leadership and ability that recognized the plan and Presence of God when He was incarnated in the womb of the Virgin. Not one great man recognized what God was doing. Then, when Jesus ministered, it was only the plain people who heard Him gladly.

I believe there is something inherent in human greatness and fame and recognition that works subtly against the quality of fine spiritual insight in the human mind. World leaders as a rule do not possess spiritual insight.

The leaders in most of the nations make a great deal of their desires and their campaigns for peace. There are few people anywhere in the world who are not interested in nations being able to live in peace and harmony. We could all wish that nations would beat their cannons and guns into implements of agriculture and peaceful production.

But such hopes for peace among nations are fleeting. The leaders who call for peace and tranquility have not done their homework in the study of the Bible and what it has to say about the future.

Even the so-called diplomats and statesmen have little knowledge and even less control over the day-to-day incidents that bring tension and violence among the nations. The story has been told of one of our own State Department officials saying to another as they arrived at the Washington offices in the morning, "Well, what is our long-range, unchanging foreign policy going to be today?"

We may smile at that, but it does illustrate the point that men and nations are completely uncertain about each new day's events. National strategy becomes sort of a game of expediency—we act or we react according to whatever another nation has done or said. In that sense, it is like a game of chess among the nations. You do not sit down and think the whole game of chess through ahead of time. You do what you are forced to do one move at a time according to the moves the other fellow makes.

I have only heard one prediction made by a world statesman in recent years that was absolutely fool-proof, and that was a remark that the next war will be fought in the future!

Well, there are no certainties, but it is sobering to realize that this present world with its great store of bombs and weapons is a powder keg, indeed. It will take only greed or lust for power or thoughtless-ness on the part of some careless man to toss the match that will set it all off again.

Where will the blame fall—on politics? on religion? on morals?

I think it is possible that these three elements of national life and world society are so intertwined that they cannot be separated.

After all, what most any nation is at its heart depends upon its religious heritage and background.

It follows that the moral life and standards of a nation will also follow the pattern of its religious instruction.

As for the ultimate politics of any given nation, you may be sure that governmental and political decisions will very likely follow the national pattern seen in the religious and moral teachings and standards.

All of these things are on the human and natural side of the growing suspicions and uncertainties among nations—and there is no prediction of man that can be counted upon as a certainty for tomorrow.

But our Lord Jesus Christ does have a certain word for us and the Bible does offer us a more sure word of prophecy.

The words of Jesus spoken to His disciples concerning the signs and evidences of His soon return at the end of the age have come down to us in the scripture record.

In this twenty-fourth chapter of Matthew's Gospel, we will note several characteristics in human society in the days just before His return.

Jesus told His followers to watch out for a growing pattern of messianic delusions.

"For many shall come in my name saying, I am Christ, and shall deceive many," Jesus warned.

He continued with the cautions that "Many false prophets shall rise and shall deceive many," and "There shall arise false Christs, and false prophets, and shall shew great signs and wonders; insomuch that, if it were possible, they shall deceive the very elect."

Now, Jesus was not saying that it would be a new kind of thing for false prophets and false Christs to appear in the end of the age, for history records that this type of fanatic and self-proclaimed prophet and redeemer has appeared quite often through the centuries. The emphasis that Jesus made was this: there will be a great number of false messiahs as though the end of the age and the perilous times that will exist will bring about an open season for this kind of false proclamation.

We may expect a greater concentration of these false prophets as the second appearing of Jesus Christ nears and the distress of nations becomes worse. These are some of the promises we will hear: "I am the Christ." "I have the answer." "I can bring peace to the world." "I can lead you into Utopia —the Promised Land." "Tomorrow the Millennium —Prosperity for all!"

A great many of these so-called "saviours" will be religious. Others are certain to be political in promise and program. Their numbers will increase as the world hastens into the vexing political, social and economic tangle of the end-time.

We note, also, that a part of the warning that Jesus gave His disciples had to do with war and violence and revolt, famines and pestilence. He said to them: "Ye shall hear of wars and rumours of wars: see that ye be not troubled: for all these things must come to pass, but the end is not yet. For nation shall rise against nation, and kingdom against kingdom: and there shall be famines, and pestilences, and earthquakes, in divers places."

In all of the teachings of Jesus concerning the conditions on earth prior to His return, there are indications of increasing dependence upon military power among the nations.

Some of us have lived long enough to see how the war and anti-war pendulum swings. Soon after World War I, there were strong anti-war movements among the people of many nations. Many preachers found it very fitting and convenient to take leading roles as pacifists and "ban-the-war" leaders.

As a result, the people of many church congregations were carried along with ministerial leaders who declared, "We outlaw war!" and who issued manifesto after manifesto to prove that mankind had learned its most important lesson with this result: "There will be no more war!"

As a result, a generation started growing up in the twenties believing that a great war could never break out again. So, we sold our unwanted scrap iron to Japan and they turned it into weapons and bombs and threw it back on us at Pearl Harbor. Almost the whole world was on fire like a tenement house and the blaze and destruction continued throughout the years of World War II. Then, the notorious A-bombs were dropped on the Japanese cities and the great war came to its costly, grisly end.

The United Nations came into being, and men and nations assured themselves once more: "Mankind has really learned his lesson this time—war must certainly be outlawed now. We will find a better way."

I ask only one question: who holds the power behind nearly every government in the world in our time?

I am sure you know the obvious answer: the military leaders!

I think back into the history of our own country. Our government is established upon the principle that the civilians—the people—will rule themselves and direct the destiny of the nation. It was long repugnant to Americans that so many nations were virtually armed camps, with generals and admirals and other military people in full control.

I suppose it is because of the kind of world in which we live, but little by little we have seen a shifting of governmental emphasis. Military men speak for the necessity of great military budgets, and generals and admirals are among those who point out the way that we must take as a nation. It is enough to make thinking men wonder if we are drifting back into the very situation in which Europe found itself before the great conflagration of World War II and the decimation that brought European nations to their knees.

Many find it easy to consider the warnings of Jesus with the casual response that war is in the nature of man, and I question whether there has ever been a time of even 365 consecutive days since the time of Christ when all the nations and all the tribes and all the divisions of mankind were actually at peace with one another.

Brethren, I do not think Jesus was cautioning us about the minor feuds and arguments between small tribal groups. Jesus could foreknow the complexities of international relations of the last days of this age; He knew full well the conditions among nations that could spawn a hellish World War III overnight.

Reading again in Matthew 24, you will find that Jesus forewarned His disciples: "And then shall many be offended, and shall betray one another, and shall hate one another."

Just think with me of all the totalitarian states and nations in today's world. What kind of control do these states have over the lives of the people, the citizens?

An important part of the totalitarian technique for control and regimentation of the people is the employment of disloyalty and hatred and betrayal within every family unit.

It is my opinion that if all of the families in Russia could have maintained complete loyalty and concern for one another within the family circles, communism would have died out in ten years. But the very basic party line is built upon so subverting the minds of the individuals that they are willing to surrender and betray their family ties as well as their former ties to church and knowledge of God.

How sad and how perverted that millions of boys and girls have been willing to betray and sell out their parents in order to get a higher mark and a higher status in the party!

As in the case of the sign of false prophets and messiahs, Jesus does not point out hatreds and betrayals as a new manifestation among humans. Jesus is making the emphasis that when this happens in the very last days before His return, it will be a great worldwide "season" for betrayal. The philosophy of treason and disloyalty is becoming an accepted and successful technique throughout the whole world.

Persecution is linked to this philosophy among modern man and Jesus said about the time of the beginning of sorrows, "Then shall they deliver you up to be afflicted, and shall kill you: and ye shall be hated of all nations for my name's sake."

I need not recite for you the well-known terror

and horror which have marked the persecutions taking place in our world since Hitler came to the European scene and turned his hatred and fury against the Jews of the world. I do not have to document for you the persecutions, regimentations and strictures which have taken place in such modern nations as Spain, Argentina and Colombia. I do not have to tell you that persecution is one of the techniques of totalitarianism, both in church and state. Jesus seemed to be pointing to a "season" for an outbroken philosophy of persecution as one of the signs of His near return.

Speaking of the last days of this age, Jesus also instructed the disciples that "because iniquity shall abound, the love of many shall wax cold."

Jesus plainly connects the increasing of iniquity in the earth with a spiritual falling away and a coldness among the people of God.

Again, we return to the fact that Jesus was not speaking of normal times among men, but of a great, concentrated "season" for sin and lawlessness as well as a "season" for coldness and callousness among the professors of religion.

I believe that Jesus meant to shake us up!

I believe that He meant for us to consider seriously what it would mean and what it would cost to keep our lamps trimmed and burning brightly in a time of great lawlessness and apostasy.

Our Lord knew that in these times there would be those in our churches who are just highly-groomed show-pieces of Christianity—middle class and well-to-do, satisfied with a religious life that costs them nothing.

Oh, yes, we do tithe! But the nine-tenths that we keep is still a hundred times more than our mothers and fathers used to have. It is right that we should tithe because it is God's work, but it does not really cost us anything—it does not bring us to the point of sacrificial giving. An old prophet of God long ago said something for us all: "Shall I offer God something that costs me nothing?"

Brethren, what has our Christian faith and witness cost us this week?

Oh, yes, you have been to church twice this week. But you would have been just as hot if you had stayed home—so it did not cost you anything. You met your friends and it was a pleasure to go to church—that did not cost you anything. You gave your tithe but you had something left to put in the bank. That did not cost you anything.

Is it not time that we face up to the fact that most of us do only those things for the Lord and for His church that we can do conveniently? If it is convenient, we will be there. If it is not convenient, we just say, "Sorry, Pastor! You will have to get someone else."

It is a generally accepted fact that most Protestant Christians serve the Lord at their own convenience. We say we believe in such things as prayer and fasting but we do not practice them unless it is convenient. Very few of us are willing to get up before daybreak as many Catholics do in order to be present in their daily services.

I am not saying that we ought to be Catholics, but I am saying that we have great throngs of professing Christians who are the slickest bunch alive in getting their religion for nothing!

We are very willing to let Jesus do all the suffering and all the sweating, all the bleeding and all the dying. It seems a great bargain to us that simply by faith we may take over all the results of His agony and death. We pat ourselves on the back for making such a good bargain, and then go galloping along to our own convenient affairs and habits.

Brethren, I realize that this message will not win any popularity prizes in the Christian ranks, but I must add this based on my observations on the current state of the church: Christianity to the average

71

evangelical church member is simply an avenue to a good and pleasant time, with a little biblical devotional material thrown in for good measure!

It is time that we begin to search our hearts and ask ourselves: "What is my Christian faith costing me? Am I offering to God something that has cost me absolutely nothing in terms of blood or sweat or tears?"

The members of many Christian churches dare to brag about being part of a "missionary-minded congregation," somehow failing to realize that it is the same old story—let the missionaries go out and suffer in the hard places. We say we are vitally interested in missions—and that seems to be true as long as it does not inconvenience us at home and the missionaries are willing to go and endure the hardships in the jungles overseas.

People in the Christian churches who put their own convenience and their own comfort and their own selfish interests ahead of the claims of the gospel of Jesus Christ surely need to get down on their knees with an open Bible—and if they are honest as they search their own hearts, they will be shocked at what they find!

Oh, brethren, have we forgotten that it was the smug, affluent, middle-class crowd that delivered Jesus to be killed when He came into our world the first time?

The poor and the oppressed and the outcasts—they heard Him gladly and they believed in Him. But how many of the poor and oppressed of our own day do we welcome into the ranks of our church fellowship with open arms?

A despised publican with his unsavory name and reputation believed in Him, and Jesus was criticized for dining with him.

But the middle-class folks, largely religious and proud and selfish, believed not and received Him not.

Well, we cannot leave these words of Jesus in

Matthew 24 without emphasizing His instructions that "this gospel of the kingdom shall be preached in all the world for a witness unto all nations; and then shall the end come."

There is no doubt that the outreach of Christian missionary activity is now greater and more extensive than at any other time in history. This should be a great rallying point for the believing children of God, and a source of strength and stability in this awful and unusual hour in which we live.

"The gospel of the kingdom shall be preached," Jesus said.

Now, let me ask you: what is a kingdom without a king? While men of this earth and the worldly kingdoms are in confusion and competition, concerned with persecutions, disloyalty and betrayal, God is in His holy temple and His throne is in heaven. In all of these situations of earth, God Almighty is trying us and testing us. He is trying the nations and the kings and the rulers of the nations.

Our Lord wants to hold us steady in these days and He asks us to look upward, for there is a kingdom, and there is a King sitting upon an eternal throne. God has promised that He will look after His people, and thus we are kept, and given His own spiritual calmness, even in the eye of the gathering storm.

Christian brethren, there will be multitudes in panic and distress because of world conditions before Christ returns as King of kings and Lord of lords. But there is a special provision for the believing Body of Christ, those who make up His church, for the angels of the Lord encamp around those who fear Him, and delivereth them. We do not yet have the heavenly understanding of all of God's promises, but there have been so many instances where true children of God in danger have been surrounded as by a wall of invisible fire that we dare to rest back on His deliverance.

I must confess that my soul delights in the words

and prophecies of our Lord Jesus, because I sense that He was able to look down the long corridor of all of the years of history, viewing the future as with a telescope, and telling us with such detail that we can be sure that He knows all things. He Himself was God and He had lived all of our tomorrows when He walked in Galilee, because He is God eternal. I delight in the inward knowledge that Jesus Christ, the Son of God and our coming Lord, will be sufficient for every situation which is yet to come to pass. We will never panic along with this present world system as long as we are fortified with our knowledge of who Jesus Christ really is.

The Word of God is the foundation of our peace and rest. Even in these dangerous and dramatic hours, "God is our refuge and strength, a very present help in trouble. Therefore will not we fear though the earth be removed, and though the mountains be carried into the midst of the sea; though the waters thereof roar and be troubled, though the mountains shake with the swelling thereof.

"There is a river, the streams whereof shall make glad the city of God, the holy place of the tabernacles of the most High. God is in the midst of her; she shall not be moved: God shall help her, and that right early.

"The heathen raged, the kingdoms were moved: he uttered his voice, the earth melted. The Lord of hosts is with us; the God of Jacob is our refuge. Come, behold the works of the Lord, . . . he maketh wars to cease unto the end of the earth."

Notice that this is the kingly strength and dominion of our Lord—not the United Nations!

He breaketh the bow and cutteth the spear in sunder. Be still and know that He is God.

In other words, get alone with God and His Word every day. I recommend that you turn off the radio and the television and let your soul delight in the fellowship and the mercies of God.

Be still and know that He is God. He will be exalted among the nations. He will be exalted in the earth. Tne Lord of hosts is with us. Fear not, little flock —it is the Father's good pleasure to give you the kingdom.

And the gates of hell cannot prevail against it!

Chapter Six

Do You Know about the Next Chapter
after the Last?

*"... Fear not ye: for I know that ye seek Jesus,
which was crucified. He is not here: for he is ris-
en, as he said. Come, see the place where the Lord
lay." Matthew 28:5-6.*

The account of the life of Jesus Christ is the only
biography known to man that does not end with
death and burial—the only record of a human life
that joyfully hastens on to the next chapter after
the last!

The book of Matthew is biography—literally, the
writing of a life. It tells the story of the birth and
life and death of a man, and by common consent,
we would include the burial. Every man knows that
when the last tattered remnants of his body are
finally taken to the grave, the last chapter of his
life will have been written. The writing of the life
ends where the life ends and at the burial the word
finis closes out the human manuscript. The word
more is no longer a consideration.

In any common biography of man, if there is any
notation after the burial, it is not true biography.
It may be editorial comment, it may be a summary
of the man's teachings, it may be eulogy—but it

is not biography. The writing of the life ends where the life ends and this is a fact by the logic of sad necessity. It holds true in every land, among all people and in the midst of every culture.

Many of the moral philosophers of the past dared to dream about a hope for tomorrow but they could never cope with the finality of death. They had always to take into account that fact that when a man is dead and buried he talks no more, he writes no more, he paints no more, he travels no more. No matter how beloved he has been, he speaks no more to his friends. The man is gone and that is the end. So, we write a respectful *finis* after the last word of the biography and it is over.

The man is gone and with the passing of the man no other chapter is possible. The last chapter has been written.

It is against this factual background that we come to the biography of Jesus. In the book of Matthew, it is a short sketch but it is a biography and it follows the common pattern of all biography.

Matthew begins with the ancestors of Jesus, back to Abraham himself, and then traces His ancestry forward to Mary. After identifying the mother of Jesus, he tells about the birth of the child, of the wise men coming from the East to see Him. Quickly Matthew proceeds to the manhood of Jesus, to the baptism with the Spirit descending like a dove and resting upon Him and preparing Him for the temptations offered by Satan in the wilderness.

The chapters that follow describe the beginning of His public ministry. Matthew records the Sermon on the Mount and then goes on to tell of the miracles of Jesus, the feeding of the 5,000, the raising of the dead, the stilling of the waves and the calming of the winds. There is a clear picture of His conflict with the hypocritical religious leaders of His day and the slow decline of His popularity with the people.

It is a striking record of the pressures of public hatred moving in to surround Jesus like the gradual falling of darkness.

Then follows the account of the arrest of Jesus by His detractors and the manner in which He was turned over to the Romans to be crucified. It is in Matthew's twenty-seventh chapter that Jesus is taken out to the hill and there, still wet with the bloody sweat of the previous night's agony, is nailed to the cross.

We learn in some detail the story of the six sad hours that followed and the humiliation of His death, the bowing of His wearied head and the words, "It is finished!" as He gave up His spirit—and He was dead.

The human biography comes to an end. Friends begged the body and tenderly placed it in a tomb and the Roman soldiers were there to place the official seal upon the grave in compliance with the Roman law. Jesus was dead—the grave was closed and sealed. His enemies were satisfied, moving on to their other interests.

There ends the human biography. This Man who had been proved to be of the seed of Abraham according to the flesh; this Man who had been declared to be the Son of God and proved so to be by His wonders and miracles and words; this Man who had struggled and fought His way with kindness and gentleness and love through the ranks of those who hated Him through three wonderful and terrible years; this Man who in love had gone out to die for His enemies is now finished. Human biography ends in the twenty-seventh chapter.

Amazingly, we find another chapter and it is there because for the first time in human history, it became necessary to get out that pen again and add another chapter—authentic biography!

Matthew 28 is not annotation! It is not composed of footnotes or summary! It is not an editorial comment or human eulogy! It is an authentic chapter in the biography of a Man who had died one chapter before.

How can this be? This Man is talking and eating, walking and making a journey with His friends on the Emmaus road. He is sharing truths about the kingdom of God and of His own coming and telling men to go into all the world preaching the gospel and witnessing of eternal life.

How can this be? His enemies and the world system had sealed the grave and written *finis*. They had satisfied themselves as well as they could that they would hear no more from this Man who had challenged their sins and their selfishness.

This is a new chapter because Jesus Christ, the Son of God, upset all of the old patterns of human life and existence. Jesus Christ took life into the grave and brought life out of the grave again and He who had been dead now lives again! For that reason, and for the first and only time in human history, it was necessary for the evangelist to add the chapter that has no ending.

Jesus Christ is alive again! This is the great truth that suddenly brought frantic confusion to those who had counted upon the old, reliable logic of death. This Man was alive again—not simply memories of Him, not just quotations from His lovely teachings, not words of commendation sent in by friends—but authentic and continuing biography!

They saw Him. They heard Him. They touched Him. They knew He was there. He stood among them. He said, "Mary!" He called His friends by name and looked at Peter and cooked fish on the sandy shore and said, "Children, have you any meat? I have some breakfast for you!"

Yes, it is an entirely new chapter. There is now a certainty of victory over death—death that had taken every man and traced him with that lipless, toothy grin; death that had waited as he went from cradle to the grave and then had written "The End."

Now it is death and the grave that are shaken with confusion for Jesus Christ is alive, having made a fool of death, and that toothless grin is as hollow now as the skull itself. Thank God there is another chapter, for He is risen. He is no longer in the grave!

We who are men must quickly ask: "What does this mean to you and me?"

Thankfully, it means for the believing and trusting Christian that the iron reign of death is ended! For those who are Christ's people, it means that the logic of death no longer applies. For Christ's believing children, it means that death is not the end—there is more to follow.

For an example of what it means, let's look at the experience of another man, the apostle Paul.

We have good biographical material here. Paul was born as other men and grew up through the maturing processes of life. He was educated at the feet of the finest teachers. He became a member of the Jewish Sanhedrin, which is equivalent to being a member of the Supreme Court in the United States. He stood high in his day as one of the orthodox Pharisees, the strictest sect among his people. But on the Damascus road he was suddenly and miraculously converted to believe and trust in the One whom he had hated. He was filled with the Holy Spirit, commissioned and sent forth to preach the gospel everywhere. He went from place to place preaching the Word, establishing churches, writing encouraging letters to the new churches.

Brought to trial one day, he was freed. On trial another day, again he was freed. Charged and tried again a third time, he was condemned.

It was then that Paul wrote a letter to a young friend, Timothy.

"The day of my departure is come and I am now ready to be offered," he wrote. He knew that death was near, so he wrote on:

"I have fought a good fight"—past perfect tense!

"I have finished my course"—past perfect tense!

"My testimony has been given. I am a martyr and a witness. I have done all that I could for Jesus. The war is over and I will take off my uniform. I have completed God's plan for me on earth."

According to the logic of death, the next words should have been "The End," for within a few days, Paul knelt on the flagstones of a Roman prison and the executioner severed his head from his body with a sword.

He had written his last testimony, but he did not say, "This is the end of Paul." Instead, he had purposely added one of those conjunctive words that speaks of a yesterday and connects it to a tomorrow.

"I have finished my course; *henceforth* . . ."

Paul's judges and jailers and executioner would have said that Paul was in no position to talk about *henceforth*—which means from here on in! Using the old logic of death, they would have said that Paul was a man with no tomorrow. His head was off. His earthly course was finished.

The fact that death was near had not caused Paul to despair. He had grasped that pen again, tired and weary as he was, and wrote in faith: "Henceforth there is laid up for me a crown of righteousness. which the Lord, the righteous judge, shall give me at that day."

Now, if it were not for that word *henceforth*, I respectfully submit that Paul could be considered one of the great fools of all time.

Consider that he was a man who had highest status in the esteem of his own nation and countrymen. He was a man of great education, culture and judgment. The historians say he undoubtedly had some wealth. He testified that he had given up all of this, counting it but refuse, turning his back on his own people, stoned one day and beaten the next, thrown into jail and bound in stocks, beset with perils and dangers, facing the schemes of those who were trying to kill him, possessing only the garments he wore and having given up everything else for Jesus' sake. When the time came for this aging man to lose his head in the Roman prison, his use of the word *henceforth* indicated that he knew he had not been a fool, and his relationship to Jesus Christ and eternal life made the sufferings in the sea and the floggings in jail and the starvation and damp rottenness in the prison seem as nothing.

Paul was testifying: "All of these things were a part of the human biography, but I am going on to another and better and eternal chapter!" For Paul, it was the blessed experience of coming to the next chapter after the last!

Thus did Paul confuse his human biographers. He knew what he was doing, for he had written: "If men do not rise again from the dead, then we are of all men most miserable"—and that is still the truth!

The promise of the resurrection makes the difference for the man who is a believing Christian. If men are not to be raised from the dead, why not eat, drink and be merry, for tomorrow we die!

But the Christian stands with Paul in the knowledge that there is another chapter because Jesus Christ is alive. We stand in faith and expectation alongside the martyrs, even though we have not been called upon to share the extremes of their sufferings. These are the believing saints of God who staunchly insisted upon the reality of another chapter after the last. They were thrown to wild beasts and were torn limb from limb. Impaled on stakes, they were allowed to die in slow agony under the sun by day and the stars by night. They were sewed into sacks and thrown over the cliffs into the waves of the ocean beneath. They were starved to death in prisons; some were driven into the wilderness to slowly die of exposure and starvation. The tongues of some were cut out; arms and hands were severed. They were fastened to carts and dragged to death through the streets while the crowds screamed with applause.

Was it worth all that?

If there had been no eternal tomorrow for those martyrs, no crown awaiting in a better land, then those torn and charred and tortured bodies would have screamed to high heaven above and hell below that Christianity is a fraud—only a cruel, treacherous story. But another chapter is waiting!

While we live in this world, we see only a few chapters of what men call earthly biography. Church history tells us that Timothy, to whom Paul wrote that final letter of triumph, died while being dragged through the streets at the tail of a cart. If that had been all for Timothy, everyone could have said, "Poor Timothy! It is too bad that he did not have sense enough to let Christianity alone!"

But you can be assured that God said to Gabriel and to those who write the records of the martyrs above: "This is not the end—just write 'More to follow!'" The divine Editor yonder in the skies knows that this is not the end of Timothy. There will be a long gap and there will be nothing written about him for a time, but this is only an episode. Another chapter follows and that chapter will have no ending!

It is God Almighty who puts eternity in a man's breast and tomorrow in a man's heart and gives His people immortality, so what you see down here really is not much. But when the bird of immortality takes to the wing, she sails on and on, over the horizon and out into the everlasting tomorrows and never comes down and never dies.

Thank God for the gracious chapter still being written, the chapter titled "Immortality." It is the chapter of God's tomorrows. It is the chapter of the *henceforths* known only to the children of God.

There is another day yet to be for there is to be a day of resurrection. I know this because there was once a Man, a lonely Man. They put Him in the grave and they sealed Him in. But the third day He arose again from the dead according to the scriptures, and ascended to the right hand of God the Father Almighty.

Besides this, I dare say that if all the books in the world were blank and were being written in by a multitude of angels until they were filled, they still would not be able to record all of the glorious deeds and words of Jesus Christ since the day evil men thought they had laid Him in the grave forever.

I want to tell you what I believe about the resurrection. When the grave that held the body of Jesus was sealed, I believe Death sat grinning beside the Roman seal, thinking, "I've got another one!" But the Life that could not stay dead broke that seal as easily as we break the seal on a letter, and Jesus walked forth, alive!

I believe that so completely that I believe it all the time. This is not an Easter "thing" that I try to believe once a year. I believe it so fully and so completely that it is a part of my being, every moment of every day. I stand humbly in this faith with all of God's dear children who are convinced that God has promised another chapter after the last.

I think often of the earthly biography and ministries of dear old Dr. R. A. Jaffray, that great missionary pioneer and statesman in the Far East and in the Pacific islands. After many fruitful years of vision, sacrifice and compassion, pressing on into all of the most forbidding and unlikely places of earth with the gospel of Jesus Christ, the last chapter of his earthly life was spent languishing in a wartime concentration camp, prisoner of the Japanese. The man who occupied the next cot while they were housed in a virtual pig pen said of Dr. Jaffray: "I never saw such godliness in any man in my lifetime."

But now, starved and sick and exhausted, Dr.

Jaffray curls up on that poor little prison cot, thousands of miles away from his nearest friends, and his human life ends. His biography says that he died. It does not say that that was the end, for Dr. Jaffray knew a gracious tomorrow in Jesus Christ and anticipated the chapter yet to come. All that he earned for himself by the grace of God will be his in the tomorrows and the complete life of Jaffray has not yet been written.

Brethren, you and I are the plain and ordinary Christians, but this shining hope relates to every one of us. We are not martyrs. We were not among the great reformers. We are not apostles.

We are the plain, everyday Christians in the family of God and there is a gracious word for us from the Saviour about our next chapter after the last. One by one we also break from the ranks and slip away.

There is nothing heroic about our passing, leaving families and friends, but then, death is never heroic and it is never kind. Death is never artistic, always much more likely to be crude and messy and humiliating.

The preacher who once stood with strength and keenness to preach the living Word of God to dying men is now in his bed, his cheeks hollow and his eyes staring, for death is slipping its chilly hand over that earthly tabernacle.

The singer whose gifts have been used to glorify God and to remind men and women of the beauty of heaven above is now hoarse, dry-lipped, whispering only a half-spoken word before death comes.

But, brethren, this is not the end. I thank God that I know that this is not all there is. My whole everlasting being, my entire personality—all that I have and all that I am are cast out on the promises of God that there is another chapter!

At the close of every obituary of His believing children, God adds the word *henceforth*! After every biography, God adds the word *henceforth*! There will be a tomorrow and this is a reason for Christian joy.

The Romans thought they had seen the last of Paul, but they were wrong. The Jews thought they had seen the last of Jesus, but they were wrong. The Japanese thought they had seen the last of Jaffray, but they were mistaken. Thank God, the Christians will be around again! This world gets rid of us, buries our bodies in the ground, charges for the trouble, and presumes that we are gone forever—but we are not! Perhaps a neighbor that hated you because you loved God will say when you die, "Well, that fellow is out of my hair. He was always giving me a tract or suggesting that I go to church. And he bored me stiff." Oh, he doesn't know that you will be around again! Yes, God's people will be around again. Paul will be back, Stephen will be back, and Timothy, who was dragged at the tail of that cart, will be back. Dr. Simpson will be back. Wesley will be back—no longer gray and weak, but in the bloom of his youth! In fact, the whole believing family of God in Christ. This is the eternal promise of God!

I recall that there was a good man of God by the name of Samuel Rutherford, whose witness shone like a star in dark England in days gone by. He was a poet, an author, and a great preacher—a man who loved Jesus probably better than any man of his times. His convictions were unpopular and he was in trouble because he refused to conform his preaching to the dictates of the state church. When he was an old man, the officials decided to try him as a criminal because he would not submit to the rules of the state church. The date of his trial was set, and he was notified by Parliament that he must appear for trial.

Rutherford knew that he was on his deathbed and so he wrote a letter in reply. He said, "Gentlemen,

I have received your summons, but before I got yours, I received one from a higher source. Before the day of my trial, I will be over there where very few kings and great men ever come. Farewell!"

That was Samuel Rutherford, witnessing to all of England that an entire new chapter awaits the Christian when our Lord says, "Welcome home!"

And "the kingly King to His white throne, my presence does command, where glory, glory, glory dwellest in Emmanuel's land." Ah, yes, there is another chapter, friends. There is a tomorrow for the people of God because there was a tomorrow for Jesus Christ our Lord. "For if we believe that Jesus died and rose again, even so them also which sleep in Jesus will God bring with him. . . . For the Lord himself shall descend from heaven with a shout, with the voice of the archangel, and with the trump of God: and the dead in Christ shall rise first: Then we which are alive and remain shall be caught up together with them in the clouds, to meet the Lord in the air: and so shall we ever be with the Lord." Then he added rather climactically, ". . . comfort one another with these words."

Ah, what a comfort this is! It is a promise to every Christian that has bid goodbye to loved ones in Christ. You will see them again! They will be around. There is another chapter, and it will have no ending. The bird of immortality is on the wing. Thank God for our faith that begins with our sins and ends with our glorification!

Chapter Seven

What Is the Supreme Sin of a Profane Society?

"He was in the world, and the world was made by him, and the world knew him not." John 1:10

The Bible tells us in a variety of ways of an ancient curse that lingers with us to this very hour —the willingness of human society to be completely absorbed in a godless world!

It is still the supreme sin of unregenerate man that, even though Jesus Christ has come into the world, he cannot feel His all-pervading Presence, he cannot see the true Light, and he cannot hear His Voice of love and entreaty!

We have become a "profane" society—absorbed and intent with nothing more than the material and physical aspects of this earthly life. Men and women glory in the fact that they are now able to live in unaccustomed luxury in expensive homes; that they can trade in shiny and costly automobiles on shinier and more costly automobiles every year; and that their tailored suits and silk and satin dresses represent an expenditure never before possible in a society of common working people.

This is the curse that lies upon modern man—he is insensible and blind and deaf in his eagerness to forget that there is a God, in his strange belief that materialism and humanism constitute the "good life."

My fellow man, do you not know that your great sin is this: the all-pervading and eternal Presence is here, and you cannot feel Him?

Are you not aware that there is a great and true Light which brightly shines—and you cannot see it?

Have you not heard within your being a tender Voice whispering of the eternal value of your soul—and yet you have said, "I have heard nothing"?

This is, in essence, the charge that John levels at human kind: Jesus Christ, the Word of God, was in the world, and the world failed to recognize Him.

Now, our word *world* in the English needs a bit of definition. In the Bible it has three distinct meanings, and two of them concern us in this passage in John's Gospel. *World* here means nature and mankind—both coming from the very same Greek word. They are used together without clear distinction, so that when the Bible says, "He was in the world, and the world knew him not," the two meanings are apparent. You must check the context to learn which meaning is which, because they come from a precise word in the original.

In the Bible, the word *world* comes from a root word meaning to tend and take care of and provide for. Then, it also means an orderly arrangement plus a decoration.

As far as I am concerned, everywhere I look in His world I see God and my soul is delighted. I look into a dry, old book that looks like a telephone directory gone mad—we call it a lexicon—and I find that in the New Testament the word *world* means "an orderly arranged system, highly decorative, which is tended, cared for, looked after and provided for." It is all there in that one word.

Anyone who knows God, even slightly, would expect God to make an orderly world because God Himself is the essence of order. God was never the author of disorder—whether it be in society, in the home, or in the mind or body of man.

I have noticed that some people let themselves go to seed in a number of ways, thinking it makes them more spiritual—but I disagree. I think it is proper to comb your hair, if you have any. I do not think it is a mark of deep inward spirituality for a man to forget that a soiled shirt is easily cleaned and that baggy trousers were originally meant to have an orderly crease in them. I am sure God is not grieved when His Christian children take a little time every day to present themselves in clean and orderly appearance.

Some of the saints of God also insist upon completely informal and spontaneous worship. I do not think our Lord is grieved by a service of worship in which we know what we are going to sing—because God is a God of order.

So the word *world* has this idea of order in it, and we can expect God to be orderly because it is necessary to His nature. The world is a mathematical world and the essence of mathematics is order—it has to be that way.

Those who have gone on to know God better will also expect that God would make a beautiful world and that is exactly what the Bible teaches. God has made an orderly and beautiful world, and He is looking after it, providing for it, and tending it.

I think this is a delightful thing—God can take an old, dry word which has been dead for hundreds of years and speak to the bones and they get up and stand and sing a solo. That is what God has done here with the word *world*.

You will think about this the next time you are asked to sing: "For the beauty of the earth, For the glory of the skies, / For the love which from our birth over and around us lies, / Lord of all, to Thee we raise This our hymn of grateful praise. / For the wonder of each hour Of the day and of the night, / Hill and vale, and tree and flower, Sun and moon, and stars of light, / Lord of all, to Thee we raise This our hymn of grateful praise."

Let me tell you that the man who wrote that was not simply having himself a poetical time. He was putting in harmonious language a truth—and that truth is that God made a world beautiful in its order.

At this point I anticipate a word of argument from Mr. Worldly Wiseman, the man who has more brains than he has heart, who thinks more than he prays, and who tries to understand and measure the unapproachable glory of God with his poor little peanut head.

He is likely to say, "Now, wait a minute. You are talking about God making the world so beautiful, but don't you know that *beauty* is a word only—a word we use to describe that which happens to please us? If a person likes the way something looks, he says it is beautiful. On the other hand, if we don't like the way something looks, we say it is ugly. So, nothing is beautiful or ugly in itself—it just depends upon whether we happen to like it or not!"

So, Mr. Worldly Wiseman tells us that this idea that God made a beautiful world is all wrong. He is of the opinion that such an idea is only the figment of an over-heated religious imagination.

Frankly, Mr. Worldly Wiseman does not frighten me by his learned criticism and I am not looking for a place to hide, because I think that he is the dumb one, after all.

Listen, brethren. God made us in His image and in His own likeness and there is a similarity between the minds of men and the mind of God, sin being excepted. Take sin out of the mind of man and the similarity to God is there because God made man in His image. I repeat—if the human race would only see that God made us in His image, we would stop

91

wallowing in the gutter and try to behave like God ordained when He made us in His own image and likeness.

When He made us in His image, part of that was mental and aesthetic so that my mind is somewhat like God's mind as soon as I get sin out of it. There is no doubt that when God makes a thing beautiful and orderly, it pleases the mind of God.

I say that it is only a half-educated man who insists that *beauty* is only a word that we give to something that happens to please us. The simple fact is that God made things to please Himself and for His pleasure they are and were created. Why should we apologize because we have the God-given ability to like what God likes and to be pleased with that which pleases God?

Now, I think that God first makes things orderly for utility. Whenever He made something in this universe it was because He had a purpose for it. I do not believe there is anything in the universe that just got here by accident. Everything in the universe has a meaning.

My father was philosophical about many things and I remember that he used to sit during the summertime and ponder why God made the mosquitoes. I still do not have the answer, but I am just a human being, and just because I do not have that answer, I am not going to accuse the Creator of making a cosmic blunder. I know the mosquito is not a blunder—he is just a pest. But God made him.

The same principle is true of a great many other things. I do not know why God does some things, but I am convinced that nothing is accidental in His universe. The fact that we do not know the reason behind some things is not basis enough for us to call them divine accidents.

If I am allowed to go into an operating room in a hospital, I find many strange and complex things all around me. I am completely ignorant as to what most of them are and how they are supposed to be used. But the surgeon knows—and all of those tools and instruments are not there by accident.

If I could step into the cab of one of the great, powerful diesel locomotives, I would be perplexed and confused trying to figure out why there are so many buttons and handles and bars. I could wreck the whole thing in a few minutes if I started pushing buttons and pressing bars. But the engineer knows—and he gets the proper results when he pushes the right buttons.

So, when God Almighty stepped into the cab of His locomotive, which we call the cosmos, He was at the controls and He has always pushed the right buttons. Just because there are things in the universe beyond my human explanation does not allow me to accuse God of making a lot of unnecessary truck to clutter up the universe. God made everything for some purpose.

I have mentioned utility in this regard. In the book of Genesis, we find that usefulness was God's first plan. God said, "Let there be light," and He saw that it was good and that it had a purpose. So He divided the light from the darkness, and called the light day and the darkness night.

God did the same thing with the waters and throughout those two chapters of Genesis there is a beautiful exercise in utility—God making an orderly world for a purpose, with everything having a reason for existence.

With God usefulness was first, and so it is with people.

Whenever a pioneering man has gone out to the undeveloped plains to get himself a homestead, a little plot of ground which is to become his home, he does not think about beauty but about utility and usefulness. He knows he must have a log house or some kind of safe dwelling before the blizzards come. You will still find many such plain, often ugly houses scattered throughout the West. It is a place to live, it is home, it is a place to rest when a man is tired. It may be primitive, but it fulfills its purpose.

In the second place, God added decoration. That is the expression that is actually in the Greek root. The word *decorative* is in it. First, He created for utility and purpose and then added decoration and beauty. There probably is a sense in which we could get along without the decoration, but it is a lot better to have it. There is that which is in the mind of God that desires to be pleased—not only satisfied. Order and usefulness and purpose bring satisfaction, but God desired that there should be beauty in His work.

I think it would be a great thing if more human beings discovered the truth that it does not cost any more to have things pleasing and beautiful than it does to have them useful and ugly. We could start out right here in our own city. You start to drive out of the city in almost any direction and you soon wonder if there is anything beautiful left in the world. Smoke stacks and smell and the sprawling apparatus for making gasoline out of crude oil—ugly, ugly, ugly! But, of course, the utility is inherent in our factories and foundries and refineries. If it were not for that kind of utility, many of you could not have driven to church—useful but not beautiful.

Well, perhaps the day will come in the millennium when we will make things beautiful as well as useful. I still think it does not cost any more to add the beauty and the pleasure and the delight. It costs no more to raise a beautiful daughter than to raise a homely daughter, and a beautiful wife does not eat any more than a homely wife.

You choose two men and give each of them a pot of paint, and one of them will turn out a masterpiece to hang in a gallery, and the other will turn out a horrible insult to the human imagination. All of that with just the same amount of paint and just the same amount of time. One is an artist and the other is a dauber.

Give two architects a free hand, each with a carload of bricks, and one will come up with a monstrosity—like some church buildings I have seen—while the other will add a touch entirely pleasing and satisfying. The costs will be the same—it is just a question of beauty in arrangement.

God could have made a river to go roaring right down to the sea—a plain, straight, ugly-looking channel. It would have fed the fish and done its job. But I think God smiled and made it to meander around under trees and around hills, a stream that catches the blue of the sky and reflects it to those nearby. People are intrigued by the meandering stream and comment, "Isn't it beautiful?" And God says, "Thank you for seeing it. I made you to see it." God is able to make things useful and beautiful. That is what the word *world* means.

Now, you say, what is this—a lecture on art?

No, it is a theological talk on what the word *world* means in the Bible—the created world which is God Almighty's decorated order which He watches and tends.

The other use of this word *world* is that which means mankind—the organized world and society of men and women.

When God reports that Christ was in the world and the world neither recognized nor knew Him, He was not referring to the created clouds and hills and rocks and rivers. He was referring to human society, the world of mankind, and it was this organized world of man that knew Him not.

John testified that God's Word, His only begotten Son, became flesh and dwelt among us. What was He doing in our kind of world, in our kind of fallen society?

Before the incarnation, He was the all-permeating

Word of God moving creatively in His universe. When Jesus Christ became man, God incarnate in a human body, He did not cease to be the all-permeating Word of God. To this very day, the all-permeating Word still fills the universe and moves among us.

How few men there are who realize His presence, who realize that they have Him to deal with. He is still the Light of the world. It is He that lighteth every man that cometh into the world. After His ascension from Olivet's mountain, He still remains as the all-permeating, vitalizing, life-giving Word operative in the universe.

What is He doing in the universe?

The scriptures tell us that "by him were all things created, that are in heaven, and that are in earth, visible and invisible, whether they be thrones, or dominions, or principalities, or powers: all things were created by him, and for him: and he is before all things (in time), and by him all things consist (or hold together)." The all-permeating Word which is in the world is the adhesive quality of the universe. That is why we do not fall apart. He is, in a very true sense, the mortar and the magnetism that holds all things together.

That is why He is here, for this is not a dead planet that we inhabit. Sin is the only dead thing. This is a living world we inhabit and it is held together by the spiritual presence of the invisible Word. He was in the world and the world was made by Him.

The scriptures continue speaking of Him: "Who being the brightness of his (God's) glory, . . . and upholding all things by the word of his power, when he had by himself purged our sins, sat down on the right hand of the Majesty on high." He is upholding all things by the word of His power.

When a little child looks up into the starry sky at night there may be a natural and childish fear that the sky will fall down. The parents laugh and pat the child on the head and apologize that he is tired—but the child is not as dumb as we might think.

Why doesn't the sky fall down? Why is it that stars and planets do not go tearing apart and ripping off into chaos?

Because there is a Presence that makes all things consist—and it is the Presence of that One who upholdeth all things by the word of His power. This is basically a spiritual explanation, for this universe can only be explained by spiritual and eternal laws. This is why the scientists can never manage to get through to the root of all things and never will, for they deal only with the things that they can see and touch and taste and mix in the experimental test tubes.

The scientist does not know how to deal with this mysterious Presence and Force that holds all things together. He can mix elements and chemicals and note the reactions that take place and then write an article and say, "I did not see God in the formula." But the scientist is only able to come up with dependable and consistent formulas because of God's faithfulness and power in holding all things together.

The scientist announces that a certain star will be in a definite place in the universe after another 2,510 years and twenty minutes! Then he sits back from his computer and boasts, "I have run God out of His world! I can predict where the stars will be in the future."

Oh, what a foolish man! The stars would all grind themselves to powder unless God in His faithfulness continues to keep them in their courses and in their systems. He upholds all things by the word of His power.

Again, we read in the scriptures: "Lift up your eyes on high, and behold who hath created these things, that bringeth out their host by number: he calleth them all by names by the greatness of his might, for that he is strong in power; not one faileth."

We lose a good deal of the expression of this passage in our English translation, but it is still one of the most beautiful in the Bible. It is a companion piece to the twenty-third Psalm, dealing with the astronomical host instead of His care for human beings.

The man of God says, "Lift up your eyes on high, and behold who hath created all these things." He is referring to that great display of shining, bright, diamond things that look down upon the country and the city and reflect on the waters of the sea. These stars yonder—who has created these things that bring out their host by number?

Why do they bring out their host?

Because they are like sheep, and this is the figure of a shepherd bringing his sheep out by number and calling them all by name, counting them as they come out and naming every one, and leading them across the green grass of the meadows and beside the still waters.

So, the shepherd-minded poet, Isaiah, saw that the starry hosts above were like a flock of sheep and that God, the great Shepherd, called and they came sailing out through the inter-stellar space as He numbered them and said, "They are all here!" Then He called them by their names, throughout the boundless universe, and because He is strong in power, not one faileth!

I believe that this can be said to be the most majestic and elevated figure of speech in the entire Bible—with no possible exception. We still know so little about the far reaches of the universe, but the astronomers tell us that the very Milky Way is not a milky way at all—but simply an incredible profusion of stars, billions of light-years away, and yet all moving in their prescribed and orderly directions.

We delight in the fact that it was God who called them all out, who knows their numbers, and He calls them all by name as a shepherd calls his sheep. What a lofty, brain-stretching illustration of what God is doing in His universe, holding all things together in proper courses and orbits.

He is that kind of Creator and God—yet the world knew Him not. That is mankind. He is still in the world, but mankind scoffs in its ignorance of Him, almost completely unaware of His revelation that the Word can be known and honored and loved by the humble human heart.

Now, the Word in His Presence can be known by mankind of the world. I am not conferring salvation upon every man by this statement. I mean to say that an awareness and consciousness of the Presence of God has often been known among men.

May I put it like this?

In the early days of America, when our founding fathers were writing constitutions and drafting laws and making history, many of the men in high places were not believing Christians. As a nation, we have been dreamy-eyed about some of those old boys and have made them out to be Christians when they were not.

I recall that Benjamin Franklin, who often said that he was not a believing Christian, suggested prayer to Almighty God at a time when the young nation was being threatened. The leaders did pray and they got out of the tight place.

Now, Franklin was not a Christian, but he believed there was a God operative in the world and he did not deny the awareness of that Presence. Daniel Webster confessed that the profoundest thought he had ever entertained in this life was his "responsibility to a holy God."

Surely, our fathers were not all fundamental Christians and many were not born again, but most of them were men who held a reverent and profound belief in the Presence of God in His world. A modern generation considers them old-fashioned and laughs at them, but they drafted far-sighted legislation and a world-renowned code of personal and national ethics and responsibilities that remain to this day.

Standing up for the awareness and consciousness of a Creator God did not save them, but it stamped them in character and manhood as apart from some of the poker-playing, whiskey-drinking rascals who have never given any thought to the idea of God and His Presence in our day. The Word is in the world and the world knows Him not—but it is possible to know.

A Moslem falls down on the ground five times a day in reverence to God in heaven—and a lot of people laugh at him. The Hindu measures himself painfully on the way to the Ganges river to bathe himself—and a lot of people comment, "How foolish can you get?"

But I would rather be a Moslem or a Hindu or a primitive tribesman living in a cootie-infested hut in Africa, kneeling before bones and feathers and mumbling some kind of home-made prayer, than to come into judgment as a self-sufficient American businessman who ruled God out of his life and out of his business and out of his home.

Many an unthinking, secular-minded American would reply: "I'm willing to take my chances!"

What foolish talk from a mortal man!

Men do not have the luxury of taking their chances—either they are saved or they are lost. Surely this is the great curse that lies upon mankind today—men are so wrapped up in their own godless world that they refuse the Light that shines, the Voice that speaks, and the Presence that pervades.

If you can stop this modern, self-sufficient man long enough to talk, he will assure you that preaching is for the down-and-out bum on Skid Row. He will assure you that he has never robbed a bank, that he is a good husband and a good citizen.

Citizenship is not the final issue with God. Morality and obeying the law are not the final issues with God. The Spirit of God tries to speak to this modern man of the great curse that lies upon his heart and life—he has become so absorbed with money and bank accounts and profit and loss and markets and loans and interest that any thought of God and salvation and eternity has been crowded out. There are dollar signs before his eyes and he would rather close another deal and make a neat profit than to make his way into the kingdom of God.

Many others in our human society are completely hooked on fame and notoriety and public attention. A well-known actress and singer recently told the press about her long career and the fame and fortune which have come to her, and she summed it all up in these words: "Fate made me what I am!"

After an entire life absorbed in a godless world and society, no better answer than some kind of esoteric, weird fate. She has lived only for the kind of fame and notice that men can give, and she would rather have her name on the marquee of a theater than to have it eternally inscribed in the Lamb's Book of Life. The Voice has been here with us, but she has never heeded it. The Light is here, but she has never seen it. The Presence is in our world, but she cannot feel it.

Money and profits, fame and fortune—and with millions of others it is a complete addiction to pleasure. Flesh contacts, nerve endings, sensuous delight, carnal joy—anything to take the seriousness out of living, anything to keep humans from sensing that there is a Presence, the Way, the Truth and the Light.

Brethren, do not charge me with acting like a mystic.

Instead, hear again these words of scripture: "In him was life; and the life was the light of men. And the light shineth in darkness; and the darkness comprehended it not." And "in the beginning was the

Word," and the Word "was in the world."

Now, there is the Word—and He is the Voice and He is the Light.

And the Word "was in the world"—there is His Presence. This is not poetry. This is the truth of God. And because our generation does not recognize the Voice and does not perceive the Light and has no sense of the Presence, we have become a profane generation. We dote on things—secular things—until we mistakenly assume that there is nothing in the universe but material and physical values. The profane man has come to the conclusion that he alone is important in this universe—thus he becomes his own god.

It is sad but true that a great and eternal woe awaits the profane and completely secular man whose only religion is in the thought that he probably is not as bad as some other man. I think that there is an Old Testament portion in the book of Job that fits modern, profane man very well: "Woe is me, that I was ever born, that my mother ever conceived me. Let the stars of the twilight of that night be as darkness. Oh, that I might have been carried from my mother's knees to the grave, where the wicked cease from troubling and the toil-worn are dressed."

I am thinking actually of men who give lip service to the church and some mental assent to religion, but they have forgotten that they were created, that they have a responsibility to God, and they have ignored Jesus Christ—His Presence, His Voice, His Light.

Actually, you can be too bright and too educated and too sophisticated, and thus fail to hear and to heed God's entreaty. But you cannot be too simple!

I was an ignorant 17-year-old boy when I first heard preaching on the street, and I was moved to wander into a church where I heard a man quoting a text: "Come unto me, all ye that labour and are heavy laden, and I will give you rest. Take my yoke upon you, and learn of me; for I am meek and lowly in heart: and ye shall find rest unto your souls."

Actually, I was little better than a pagan, but with only that kind of skimpy biblical background, I became greatly disturbed, for I began to feel and sense and acknowledge God's gracious Presence. I heard His Voice—ever so faintly. I discerned that there was a Light—ever so dimly.

I was still lost, but thank God, I was getting closer. The Lord Jesus knows that there are such among us today, of whom He says: "Ye are not far from the kingdom of God."

Once again, walking on the street, I stopped to hear a man preaching at a corner, and he said to those listening: "If you do not know how to pray, go home and get down and ask, 'God, have mercy on me, a sinner.' "

That is exactly what I did, and in spite of the dispensational teachers who tell me that I used the wrong text, I got into my Father's house. I got my feet under my Father's table. I got hold of a big spoon and I have been enjoying my Father's spiritual blessings ever since.

Actually, I have paid no attention to those brethren pounding on the window outside, shouting at me and beckoning to me, "Come on out of there, boy. You got in by the wrong door!"

Dispensations or not, God has promised to forgive and satisfy anyone who is hungry enough and concerned enough and anxious enough to cry out, "Lord, save me!"

When Peter was starting to sink under those waters of Galilee, he had no time to consult the margin of someone's Bible to find out how he should pray. He just prayed out of his heart and out of his desperation, "Lord, save me!" And his Lord answered.

Brethren, why don't we just let our hearts do the praying? If a man will just get his heart down on its knees, he will find that there is an awful lot that he does not need to know to receive Jesus Christ!

He is here now. "The Word became flesh and dwelt among us." He went away in His human body, but He is still with us—the everlasting, all-permeating Word—still with us to save! He only waits for a child-like prayer from a humble and needy heart—"Oh, Lamb of God, I come, I come!"

Chapter Eight

Is It True that Man Lost His Franchise to the Earth?

"In my Father's house are many mansions: if it were not so, I would have told you. I go to prepare a place for you." John 14:2

When the followers of Jesus Christ lose their interest in heaven they will no longer be happy Christians and when they are no longer happy Christians they cannot be a powerful force in a sad and sinful world. It may be said with certainty that Christians who have lost their enthusiasm about the Saviour's promises of heaven-to-come have also stopped being effective in Christian life and witness in this world.

I still must lean in the direction of the old camp meetings songs in which happy and effective Christians gloried in the promises of a heavenly home where there is no need of sun or moon because the Lamb is the light thereof! Those enthusiastic souls were much nearer the truth than today's dignified theologians who discourage us from being too pragmatic about the joyful prospects of our future home.

It is very clear in Bible revelation that God created all things to display His own glory and then ordained that man should be the supreme instrument through which He might display those glories.

It was for that reason that man was made in God's own image and likeness—a description of man alone and a term never used concerning any other of God's creatures.

There is no doubt that man was created for this earth. For reasons known only to God, God chose the earth as man's sphere of activity. He made man of the dust of the ground and adapted our nature to earth's conditions.

Did you ever stop to thank God that you are adapted to the environment around you? You could not live on the moon. You could not live on any of the heavenly bodies, as far as we know, but you can live on this earth. God adapted our natures so we can live here even as He adapted the fish to the water and the birds to the air. So, He made the earth to be our home and our garden, our workshop and our bed.

But, as we know, the conditions of the earth which God made specifically for mankind were not those we know today. It is the same body geographically—but in its creation it was the Eden of perfect love, where God walked with men in peace and beauty. In the beauty of His living presence God created the heaven and the earth, and the downshining of God upon the earth made the very fields and meadows and arbors and grassy places glorious and heavenly.

Then came the fall of man.

No one should ever be able to argue and persuade us that the fall of man from his glory and perfection was not real. Many already challenge our right to believe that man is a fallen creature—but that is exactly what he is.

The fall of man set in motion a great moral shock. It was a shock felt in the heart of God and in all of earth's circumference and certainly in the whole nature of man—body and soul and mind and spirit.

It is not too much to say that this disaster that we describe as the fall of man was of a magnitude never known before in all of the vast creation of God. It was of greater magnitude than the fall of angels whom the Bible says kept not their first estate but left their proper habitation and because of this were hurled down into everlasting darkness and judgment.

This is the magnitude of man's fall and man's sin—man lost his God-given franchise to this earth, and thus can remain here only for a brief time!

Bernard of Cluny wrote of man: "Brief life is here thy portion"—but that was not God's plan and desire for man in the beginning. God adapted man to the earth and the earth to man when He said, "Increase and multiply and replenish the earth, and subdue it . . . it shall be thine . . . thou shalt eat of every tree of the garden, and the herbs of the field shall be thine for food."

Then man sinned and lost his franchise and it was necessary for the Creator to say: "You can now stay only for a little while." And during that little while that he is staying here, he suffers the loss of Eden with its paradise of peace and love, while the earth itself suffers pollution. Sickness and disease must be reckoned with, toil and sorrow, and mortality and death itself.

Someone is likely to challenge the listing of both mortality and death as though the two are identical.

Actually, mortality is the sentence of death. Death is the carrying out of the sentence of mortality. They are not the same. Death is the final act— man's mortality lies in his knowledge that he can never escape!

In history there is the account of a famous political prisoner standing before his judge. Asked if he had anything to say before sentence was pronounced, the man said "No." The judge intoned, "I therefore pronounce that on a certain day you shall be hanged by the neck until death. I sentence you to die." It was then that the prisoner spoke: "Your honor, nature has sentenced you to die, as well." In dignity, he turned and walked away to his cell.

For mankind, the earth has become the symbol of death and mortality, of the loss of Eden with all of its joys and the loss of paradise of peace and the presence of God. That is why the earth does not have a good reputation with believing Christians. The more mature we become in spiritual life and in dedication to Christ, the less we desire the things of this earth. It has become plain to us that this earth, with its darkness and shadows, with its empty promises and disappointments, with its lies and deceptions, its pains and sorrows and griefs that cry out in the night, is a symbol of everything that is unlike God.

In the very face of this truth, the Christian still knows for certain that God has not forgotten him. Man who was made in the image of God has not been forsaken—God promised a plan to restore that which had been made in His image.

Those angels that rebelled and did not keep their first estate have no redeemer, for they were not made in the image and likeness of God. Those strange, weird creatures we call demons were not made in His image. They have no redeemer. Lucifer, the son of the morning, who said, "I will be like God," has no redemption and salvation from his fall, for he was not created in God's image.

Only that creature whom he called "man" did God make in His own image and likeness. So, when man failed and sinned and fell, God said, "I will go down now."

God came down to visit us in the form of a man, for in Jesus Christ we have the incarnation, "God manifest in the flesh." God Himself came down to this earthly island of man's grief and assumed our loss and took upon Himself our demerits, and in so doing, redeemed us back unto Himself. Jesus Christ, the King of glory, the everlasting Son of the Father, in His victory over sin and death opened the kingdom of heaven to all believers!

That is what the Bible teaches. That is what the Christian church believes. It is the essence of the doctrines of the Christian church relating to atonement and salvation.

Beyond His death and resurrection and ascension, the present work of Jesus Christ is twofold. It is to be an advocate above—a risen Saviour with high priestly office at the throne of God; and the ministry of preparing a place for His people in the house of His Father and our Father, as well.

Now, it must be said that sin necessitates a separation of body and soul. While it is proper to say that man is made for the earth, it is actually necessary to say that man's body is made for the earth. It was his body that was taken from the dust of the ground, for man became a living soul when God breathed into his nostrils the breath of life. The image of God was not in the body of the man, but in the spirit that made him man. The body is simply the instrument through which the soul manifests itself down here—that is all.

It is out of this context, however, that we need the caution that the worth and value of our human body should not be played down.

God has seen fit to give us this amazingly delicate and adaptable and beautiful instrument—the human body. If there had been no sin, there would never have been even the remotest shadow of doubt concerning the beauty, the dignity and usefulness of the body.

We should not think it is humility to berate and cry down this body which God has given us. It serves us well, but it has no power in itself. It has no will of its own. The body cannot express affection or emotion. The human body has no thought processes. Our human thought processes lie within the soul, in the human mind, in the human spirit. But God has ordained that it is through the instrument of the body that our ability to think shines forth and expresses itself.

The apostle Paul gave us plain teaching in this regard when he said: "Let not sin therefore reign in your mortal body, that ye should obey it in the lusts thereof. Neither yield ye your members as instruments of unrighteousness unto sin: but yield yourselves unto God, as those that are alive from the dead, and your members as instruments of righteousness unto God .... But God be thanked, that ye were the servants of sin, but ye have obeyed from the heart that form of doctrine which was delivered you. Being then made free from sin, ye became the servants of righteousness. I speak after the manner of men because of the infirmity of your flesh: for as ye have yielded your members servants to uncleanness and to iniquity unto iniquity; even so now yield your members servants to righteousness unto holiness."

It is important that we realize the human body is simply an instrument, because there are those who have taught that Christ could not be God in the flesh because the body is evil and God would not thus come in contact with evil.

The false premise there is the belief that the human body is evil. There is no evil within inert matter. There is nothing evil in matter itself. Evil lies in the spirit. Evils of the heart, of the mind, of the soul, of the spirit—these have to do with man's sin, and the only reason the human body does evil is because the human spirit uses it to do evil.

For example, a gun lying in a drawer is a harmless thing and of itself has no power to injure or harm. When an angry man takes the gun in his hand he becomes the lord of that instrument. The instrument is said to inflict pain and death, but that is not really true. The motive and intent and the direction to harm is in the will and the emotion of the man and he uses the gun as an instrument.

Men have been known to use their hands to choke others to death in the high pitch of human anger and jealousy and lust. The hands kill—but yet the hands do not really kill. Take the direction of that distorted spirit away from these hands and they will lie inert until they rot.

No, sin does not lie in the human body. There is nothing in the human body that is bad. Sin lies in the will of the man and when the man wills to sin, he uses his body as a harmless, helpless instrument to do his evil purposes.

The fact that the body cannot act apart from the spirit of man is good truth and we cite it here as prelude to the fact that there are many mansions in our Father's house in heaven, in the New Jerusalem, in the city four-square.

I think Christians ought to know and understand God's reasoning and philosophy behind His eternal provision for His children. I am not happy with the attitude of some Christians who are little more than parrots concerning the truths of God.

Some people think it is spiritual just to accept all of the dogmas without any real thought or comprehension—"Yes, I believe it. The Bible says it and I believe it."

We are supposed to be mature and growing Christians, able to give an answer with comprehension concerning our faith. We are supposed to be more than parrots.

The parrot in the pet shop can be taught to quote John 3:16 or portions of the Apostles' Creed if you give him tid-bits as a reward. If all we want is to have someone feed truth into us without knowing or understanding why it is like it is, then we are simply Christian parrots saying "I believe! I believe!"

I think we Christians should spend a lot more time thinking about the meaning and implications of our faith, and if we ask God Almighty to help us, we will know why He has dealt with us as He has and why the future holds bright promise for God's children.

So, the scriptures do support our belief that while the body cannot act apart from the spirit, it is possible for the spirit to act apart from the body.

Do you remember what the Apostle wrote in First Peter 3:18? Peter said that "Christ also hath once suffered for sins, the just for the unjust, that he might bring us to God, being put to death in the flesh, but quickened by the Spirit: By which also he went and preached unto the spirits in prison; which sometime were disobedient, when once the longsuffering of God waited in the days of Noah."

Now, that tells us very plainly that Christ Jesus was actively doing something specific and intelligent and creative while His body was resting in Joseph's new tomb. The body could not move, it could do nothing apart from His spirit; but while the body was still in the tomb of Joseph, His spirit was busy and active about His Father's business, preaching to the spirits in prison, which aforetime were disobedient in the days of Noah.

"But, that was Jesus the Christ," you may say. "What about others?"

Let me refer you to the sixth chapter of Revelation. beginning at verse nine:

"When he had opened the fifth seal, I saw under the altar the souls of them that were slain for the word of God, and for the testimony which they held: and they cried with a loud voice, saying, How long, O Lord, holy and true, dost thou not judge and avenge our blood on them that dwell on the earth? And white robes were given unto every one of them, . . . that they should rest yet for a little season, until their fellowservants also and their brethren, that should be killed as they were, should be fulfilled."

We notice that here were some souls, tucked up safely under the altar of God, and they were the souls of the men and women who had been slain. What was slain? The bodies, not the souls. Jesus told His disciples: "Fear not them which kill the body, rather fear him which is able to destroy soul and body in hell."

It is interesting and profitable for us to note what these souls were doing. We find them intelligent, we find they had memory, we find they prayed, we find that they have a sense of justice. Further, we note their knowledge that God is holy and true, that men dwell on the earth and they know that God is a judge who avenges Himself and those whose blood had been shed. All of these things were true of the souls of those whose bodies had been slain.

So, it is fully possible for your spirit to act without your body, but it is not possible for your body to act without your spirit. Further, I would suggest that you do not try to demonstrate the actions of your spirit without your body while in this life. God does not suggest it in this life.

The spiritists, so-called mediums, tappers, peepers and glass-ball gazers try to loose the spirit and talk about it soaring off and freeing man here below. No, no, not that! Ghosts and wizards and spooks—all of that activity is under the stern interdiction of the God Almighty. God expects us to stay inside these bodies now, serving Him until that day when the Lord releases us and our spirits can soar away.

Why can't we take our bodies along in that day? I say it is because of sin. Man's sin has separated us in terms of our spirits and bodies.

At this point in our thinking, the question must occur: "If our bodies are separated at death, why have a heaven at all?" Some have actually taken the position at this point that there is no such thing as heaven—that the earth is to be man's heaven, and that man will receive immortality and the earth will be his sphere of operation.

That may be an interesting thought from the human point of view, but that is not what the Bible teaches!

The Bible has a definite answer for us. It tells us that God made us in His image in giving us His breath, making us living souls. Then, in that indescribable calamity, that moral disaster of the fall, all men lost the blessings of that first estate and have felt the sad results of that fall ever since in spirit, soul, mind and body.

The Bible answer includes God sending His Son to redeem us and to make us whole again. Some people seem to think that Jesus came only to reclaim us or restore us so that we could regain the original image of Adam. Let me remind you that Jesus Christ did infinitely more in His death and resurrection than just undoing the damage of the fall. He came to raise us into the image of Jesus Christ, not merely to the image of the first Adam. The first man Adam was a living soul, the second man Adam was a life-giving Spirit. The first man Adam was made of the earth earthy, but the second man is the Lord from heaven!

Redemption in Christ, then, is not to pay back dollar-for-dollar or to straighten man out and restore him into Adamic grace. The purpose and work of redemption in Christ Jesus is to raise man as much above the level of Adam as Christ Himself is above the level of Adam. We are to gaze upon Christ, not Adam, and in so doing are being transformed by the Spirit of God into Christ's image.

So, we can say that earth may have been good enough for that creature who was created from the dust and clay, but it is not good enough for the living soul who is redeemed by royal blood! Earth was fit and proper to be the eternal dwelling place for that creature who was made by God's hand, but it is not

114

appropriate nor sufficient to be the eternal dwelling place of that redeemed being who is begotten of the Holy Ghost. Every born-again Christian has been lifted up—lifted up from the level of the fallen Adamic race to the heavenly plane of the unfallen and victorious Christ. He belongs up there!

But, in the meantime, sin separates body and soul. That is why the Lord Jesus Christ, as He was about to leave the earth after His resurrection, told His disciples: "In my Father's house are many mansions . . . I go to prepare a place for you. And if I go and prepare a place for you, I will come again, and receive you unto myself; that where I am, there ye may be also."

It is an amazing thing that Jesus Christ claimed that He never left the bosom of the Father. He said the Son of Man, who is in the bosom of the Father, hath declared it. While Jesus was upon earth, walking as a man among men, by the mystery of the ever-present God and the indivisible substance of the Deity, He could remain in the bosom of the Father, and He did.

So, you and I are to be elevated and promoted. Let us not forget that it was the Lord God Almighty who made man and blew into him the breath of life so that he became a living soul. That was man—and then in redemption God raised him infinitely above that level, so that now we hear the Lord and Saviour promising, "I have gone to prepare a place for you." In the time of our departure, the body that He gave us will disintegrate and drop away like a cocoon, for the spirit of the man soars away to the presence of God. The body must await that great day of resurrection at the last trump, for Paul says, "The dead shall be raised incorruptible, and we shall all be changed."

With the promises of God so distinct and beautiful, it is unbecoming that a Christian should make such a fearful thing of death. The fact that we Christians do display a neurosis about dying indicates that we are not where we ought to be spiritually. If we had actually reached a place of such spiritual commitment that the wonders of heaven were so close that we longed for the illuminating Presence of our Lord, we would not go into such a fearful and frantic performance every time we find something wrong with our physical frame.

I do not think that a genuine, committed Christian ever ought to be afraid to die. We do not have to be because Jesus promised that He would prepare a proper place for all of those who shall be born again, raised up out of the agony and stress of this world through the blood of the everlasting covenant into that bright and gracious world above.

Notice that Jesus said, "In my Father's house are many mansions." If it is His Father's house, it is also our Father's house because the Lord Jesus is our elder brother. Jesus also said, "I go to my Father and your Father—my God and your God." If the Father's house is the house of Jesus, it is also the house of all of His other sons and daughters.

Yes, we Christians are much better off than we really know—and there are a great many things here below that we can get along without and not be too shaken about it if we are honestly committed to the promises concerning the Father's house and its many dwelling places. It is one of the sad commentaries on our times that Christians can actually be foolish enough to get their affections so centered upon the things of this earth that they forget how quickly their little time in this body and upon this earth will flee away.

I am sure that our Lord is looking for heavenly-minded Christians. His Word encourages us to trust Him with such a singleness of purpose that He is able to deliver us from the fear of death and the uncertainties of tomorrow. I believe He is up there preparing me a mansion—"He is fixing up a mansion which shall forever stand; for my stay shall not be transient in that happy, happy land!"

Read again what John said about his vision of the future to come.

"I saw a new heaven and a new earth: for the first heaven and the first earth were passed away; and there was no more sea. And I John saw the holy city, the new Jerusalem, coming down from God out of heaven, prepared as a bride adorned for her husband."

Brethren, I say that it is just too bad that we have relegated this passage to be read mostly at funeral services. The man who was reporting this was not on his way to a funeral—he was on his way to the New Jerusalem!

He continued: "And I heard a great voice out of heaven saying, Behold, the tabernacle of God is with men, and he will dwell with them, and they shall be his people, and God himself shall be with them, and be their God. And God shall wipe away all tears from their eyes; and there shall be no more death, neither sorrow, nor crying, neither shall there be any more pain: for the former things are passed away."

John then describes that great and beautiful city having the glory of God, with her light like unto a stone that was most precious, even like as jasper, clear as crystal.

"And I saw no temple therein: for the Lord God Almighty and the Lamb are the temple of it. And the city had no need of the sun, neither of the moon, to shine in it: for the glory of God did lighten it, and the Lamb is the light thereof."

Ah, the people of God ought to be the happiest people in all the wide world! People should be coming to us constantly and asking the source of our joy and delight—redeemed by the blood of the Lamb, our yesterdays behind us, our sin under the blood forever and a day, to be remembered against us no more forever. God is our Father, Christ is our

117

Brother, the Holy Ghost our Advocate and Comforter. Our Brother has gone to the Father's house to prepare a place for us, leaving with us the promise that He will come again!

Don't send Moses, Lord, don't send Moses! He broke the tables of stone.

Don't send Elijah for me, Lord! I am afraid of Elijah—he called down fire from heaven.

Don't send Paul, Lord! He is so learned that I feel like a little boy when I read his epistles.

O Lord Jesus, come yourself! I am not afraid of Thee. You took the little children as lambs to your fold. You forgave the woman taken in adultery. You healed the timid woman who reached out in the crowd to touch You. We are not afraid of You!

Even so, come, Lord Jesus!

Come quickly!

Chapter Nine

Will You Allow God to Reproduce Christ's Likeness in You?

"I am crucified with Christ: nevertheless I live; yet not I, but Christ liveth in me: and the life which I now live in the flesh I live by the faith of the Son of God, who loved me, and gave himself for me." Galatians 2:20

There seems to be a great throng of professing Christians in our churches today whose total and amazing testimony sounds about like this: "I am thankful for God's plan in sending Christ to the cross to save me from hell."

I am convinced that it is a cheap, low-grade and misleading kind of Christianity that impels people to rise and state: "Because of sin I was deeply in debt—and God sent His Son, who came and paid all my debts."

Of course believing Christian men and women are saved from the judgment of hell and it is a reality that Christ our Redeemer has paid the whole slate of debt and sin that was against us.

But what does God say about His purposes in allowing Jesus to go to the cross and to the grave? What does God say about the meaning of death and resurrection for the Christian believer?

Surely we know the Bible well enough to be able

to answer that: God's highest purpose in the redemption of sinful humanity was based in His hope that we would allow Him to reproduce the likeness of Jesus Christ in our once-sinful lives!

This is the reason why we should be concerned with this text—this testimony of the apostle Paul in which he shares his own personal theology with the Galatian Christians who had become known for their backslidings. It is a beautiful miniature, shining forth as an unusual and sparkling gem, an entire commentary on the deeper Christian life and experience. We are not trying to take it out of its context by dealing with it alone; we are simply acknowledging the fact that the context is too broad to be dealt with in any one message.

It is the King James version of the Bible which quotes Paul: "I am crucified with Christ." Nearly every other version quotes Paul as speaking in a different tense: "I have been crucified with Christ," and that really is the meaning of it: "I have been crucified with Christ."

This verse is quoted sometimes by people who have simply memorized it and they would not be able to tell you what Paul was really trying to communicate. This is not a portion of scripture which can be skipped through lightly. You cannot skim through and pass over this verse as many seem to be able to do with the Lord's prayer and the twenty-third Psalm.

This is a verse with such depth of meaning and spiritual potential for the Christian believer that we are obligated to seek its full meaning—so it can become practical and workable and liveable in all of our lives in this present world.

It is plain in this text that Paul was forthright and frank in the matter of his own personal involvement in seeking and finding God's highest desires and provision for Christian experience and victory. He was not bashful about the implications of his own personality becoming involved with the claims of Jesus Christ.

Not only does he plainly testify, "I have been crucified," but within the immediate vicinity of these verses, he uses the words *I, myself* and *me* a total of 14 times.

There certainly is, in the Bible, a good case for humility in the human personality, but it can be overdone.

We have had a dear missionary veteran among us from time to time. He is learned and cultured—and overly modest. With a great wealth of missionary exploits and material to tell, he has always refused to use any first person reference to himself.

When asked to tell about something that happened in his pioneer missionary life, he said: "One remembers when one was in China and one saw . . ." That seems to be carrying the idea of modesty a bit too far, so I said to him, in a joking way, that if he had been writing the Twenty-third Psalm, it would likely read: "The Lord is one's shepherd, one shall not want; he maketh one to lie down in green pastures. He leadeth one . . ."

I believe Paul knew that there is a legitimate time and place for the use of the word *I*. In spiritual matters, some people seem to want to maintain a kind of anonymity, if possible. As far as they are concerned, someone else should take the first step. This often comes up in the manner of our praying, as well. Some Christians are so general and vague and uninvolved in their requests that God Himself is unable to answer. I refer to the man who will bow his head and pray: "Lord, bless the missionaries and all for whom we should pray. Amen."

It is as though Paul says to us here: "I am not ashamed to use myself as an example. I have been crucified with Christ. I am willing to be pin-pointed."

Only Christianity recognizes why the person who is without God and without any spiritual perception

121

gets in such deep trouble with his own ego. When he says *I*, he is talking about the sum of his own individual being, and if he does not really know who he is or what he is doing here, he is beseiged in his personality with all kinds of questions and problems and uncertainties.

Most of the shallow psychology religions of the day try to deal with the problem of the ego by jockeying it around from one position to another, but Christianity deals with the problem of *I* by disposing of it with finality.

The Bible teaches that every unregenerated human being will continue to wrestle with the problems of his own natural ego and selfishness. His human nature dates back to Adam. But the Bible also teaches with joy and blessing that every individual may be born again, thus becoming a "new man" in Christ.

When Paul speaks in this text, "I have been crucified," he is saying that "my natural self has been crucified." That is why he can go on to say, "Yet I live"—for he has become another and a new person —"I live in Christ and Christ lives in me."

It is this first *I*, the natural me, which stands confronted with the just anger of God. God cannot acknowledge and accept me as a natural and selfish man—I am unregenerate and an alien, the complete essence of everything that is anti-God!

I know there are men and women who dismiss the idea of anything being anti-God or anti-Christ. They are not willing to pay any heed to the teachings of scripture relative to prophecy and eschatology.

Nevertheless, it is a biblical fact that whatever does not go through the process of crucifixion and transmutation, passing over into the new creation, is anti-Christ. Jesus said that all of that which is not with Christ is against Christ—those who are not on His side are against Him. We do not quite know what to do with those words of Christ, so we try to evade or work them over to a smooth, new version, but Jesus said, "If you do not gather with me, you scatter abroad."

There is a great hue and cry throughout the world today on behalf of tolerance and much of it comes from a rising spirit of godlessness in the nations. The communist nations, themselves the most intolerant, are preaching and calling for tolerance in order to break down all of the borders of religion and embarrass the American people with our social and racial problems.

This is the situation of the people of God: the most intolerant book in all the wide world is the Bible, the inspired Word of God, and the most intolerant teacher that ever addressed himself to an audience was the Lord Jesus Christ Himself.

On the other hand, Jesus Christ demonstrated the vast difference between being charitable and being tolerant. Jesus Christ was so charitable that in His great heart He took in all the people in the world and was willing to die even for those who hated Him.

But even with that kind of love and charity crowning His being, Jesus was so intolerant that He taught: "If you are not on my side, you are against me. If you do not believe that I am he, you shall die in your sins." He did not leave any middle ground to accommodate the neutral who preach tolerance. There is no "twilight zone" in the teachings of Jesus— no place in between.

Charity is one thing but tolerance is quite another matter.

Tolerance easily becomes a matter of cowardice if spiritual principles are involved, if the teachings of God's Word are ignored and forgotten.

Suppose we take the position of compromise that many want us to take: "Everyone come, and be saved if you want to. But if you do not want to be saved, maybe there is some other way that we can find for you. We want you to believe in the Lord Jesus Christ if you will, but if you do not want to, there may be a possibility that God will find some other way for you because there are those who say that there are many ways to God."

That would not be a spirit of tolerance on our part—it would be downright cowardice. We would be guilty with so many others of a spirit of compromise that so easily becomes an anti-God attitude.

True Christianity deals with the human problem of the self life, with the basic matter of "me, myself and I." The Spirit of God deals with it by an intolerant and final destruction, saying, "This selfish *I* cannot live if God is to be glorified in this human life."

God Himself deals with this aspect of human nature—the sum of all our proud life—and pronounces a stern condemnation upon it, flatly and frankly disapproving of it, fully and completely rejecting it.

And what does God say about it?

"I am God alone, and I will have nothing to do with man's selfish ego, in which I find the essence of rebellion and disobedience and unbelief. Man's nature in its pride of self and egotism is anti-God —and sinful, indeed!"

It is in this matter of how to deal with man's proud and perverse and sinful human nature that we discover two positions within the framework of Christianity.

One position is that which leans heavily upon the practice of psychology and psychiatry. There are so-called Christian leaders who insist that Jesus came into the world to bring about an adjustment of our ego, our selfishness, our pride, our perversity. They declare that we may become completely adjusted to life and to one another by dealing with the complexes and the twisted concepts that we have gotten into because our mothers scolded us when we were babies! So, there are thousands of referrals as the clergymen shift our problems from the church to the psychiatric couch.

On the other hand, thank God, the Bible plainly

says that Jesus Christ came to bring an end of *self*
—not to educate it or tolerate it or polish it! No one
can ever say that Jesus Christ came to tell us how
to cultivate our natural ego and pride. Jesus never
taught that we could learn to get along with the big,
proud *I* in our lives by giving it a love for Bach
and Beethoven and Da Vinci.

Paul outlined the full spiritual remedy: "I am
crucified with Christ . . . and the life which I now
live in the flesh I live by the faith of the Son of
God, who loved me, and gave himself for me."

This is a decision and an attitude of faith and
commitment called for in the life of every believing Christian.

When we see that Jesus Christ came into the world
to deal effectively and finally with our life of self
and egotism and pride, we must take a stand.

With God's help, we say to that big *I*
in our nature: "This is as far as you go—you are
deposed. You are no longer to be in control!" In
true repentance and in self-repudiation, we may turn
our backs on the old self life. We may refuse to
go along with it any longer. We have the right and
the power to desert its ranks and cross over to spiritual victory and blessing on Emmanuel's side, walking joyfully under the banner of the cross of Jesus
Christ from that hour on.

This is what it means to deal with and finally
dispose of the "old man," the old life of self, which
is still causing problems in so many Christian lives.
We take a place of actual identification with Jesus
Christ in His crucifixion, burial, and resurrection.

In the Christian life, that is what baptism is supposed to mean, but sad to say, baptism is nothing
but a quick dip to the average person because that
one does not know what baptism represents. He does
not know that baptism genuinely ought to be an outward and visible testimony of a spiritual and inward
transformation that has taken place; a symbol de-

125

claring that the old selfish and perverse human nature is repudiated in humility, and put away, crucified, declared dead!

That is what baptism should mean to the believer —death and burial with Christ, then raised with Him in the power of His resurrection! It can happen apart from water baptism of any mode, but that is what water baptism should indicate. It should set forth that identification with the death and resurrection of Jesus Christ just as a wedding ring witnesses and sets forth the fact that you are married.

Now, it is impossible to bring together and synchronize these two positions concerning the old life and nature of self. I do not believe that we are ever obliged to dovetail these two positions. Either the Lord Jesus Christ came to bring an end of self and reveal a new life in spiritual victory, or He came to patch and repair the old self—He certainly did not come to do both!

I expect someone to say, "We are interested in spiritual victory and blessing in our group, but our approach doesn't agree with yours at all!"

In answer I can only say that on the basis of the Word of God, true identification with Jesus Christ in His death, burial and resurrection will lead men and women to Christ-likeness. God has never promised to work out His image in us in a variety of ways according to the inclinations of our own group. Forming the likeness to Jesus Christ in human lives and personalities is something that He does alike in all groups and all conferences and all fellowships around the world regardless of what they may be called.

There really is no way to patch up and repair the old life of self. The whole burden of New Testament theology insists that the old human self is ruined completely. It has no basic goodness, it holds to false values and its wisdom is questionable, to say the least. It is the new self in Christ Jesus—the new man in Christ—which alone must live. Onward from the point of this commitment, we must reckon ourselves indeed to have died unto sin, to be alive unto God in Christ Jesus.

But the natural self, the natural "I, myself and me," is continually taking inventory, seeking and hoping to find some human help in trying to forget and escape the guilty past, something that will make it more acceptable in God's sight, something that will enable it to develop to the fullest the potential of its nature.

Part of man's natural frustration is the inner feeling and realization that he is never measuring up and achieving to the full potential given him in creation. Actually, I believe God has created each one of us with a master blueprint representing His highest desires for the use of our many capacities in this life.

With God's blueprint stretching forth in all directions, what usually happens to the human life and personality? Well, we may see a utilitarian little house or shack there in the middle of it, and after a few years of hard work, an addition of some kind, but the outreach of our human personality which we picture in this way never stretches out to the limits of the blueprint.

The human nature in its striving and its groping has never been able to finally roll up the blueprint, put it away on the shelf, and say, "Thank God, my earthly existence is everything God desired it to be! The last wall has been raised, that final arch is complete, the roof is without a flaw—it is a habitation that can be considered to be perfect!"

The potential and the abilities of man's mighty nature are almost limitless—but we have to add, not quite! I am always stirred in my being to consider all that created man can do, the great powers and ability to think, the powers of imagination

127

and creativity. Yet, if men and women do not find a way to properly use all of those powers and talents and gifts in bringing praise and honor and glory to God the Creator and the Redeemer, they are still not what they ought to be.

I believe there is a subconscious desire deep within every human being to realize and utilize his full potential—the desire to live a full and complete life, which often means the hope of escaping the past and the ability to face the future in confidence.

But what do men and women actually find when they look into their own hearts in this quest? They find nothing that measures up to their dreams and hopes. They find that they possess nothing of eternal value. They find that they know nothing with any certainty. They find that they can do nothing which is acceptable in the sight of a holy God.

Human beings continue to lean on a variety of crutches to support the ego, to nourish the pride, to cover the obvious defects in human existence. Many have believed that continuing education would provide that missing link between personality and potential. Many have turned to the pursuits of philosophies; others to cultural achievements. Ancestry and environment and status occupy many more.

But the ability to brag about human ancestors, to point with pride to the nation of our descent or the cultural privileges we have known—these do not transform and change and regenerate the human nature. Regardless of our racial strains, regardless of our cultural and educational advantages, we are all alike as human beings. In my own nature, I am nothing. Of myself, I know nothing. In God's sight, without His help and His enabling, I have nothing and I can do nothing.

But the inventory of the new man in Christ Jesus is so different! If he has found the meaning of commitment, the giving up of self to be identified with Jesus Christ in His crucifixion and death, he discovers in an entirely new measure the very presence of Christ Himself!

This new person has made room for the presence of Christ, so there is a difference in the personal inventory. It is no longer the old do-nothing, know-nothing, be-nothing, have-nothing person! That old assertive self died when the crucified and risen Saviour was given His rightful place of command and control in the personality. The old inventory cried out: "How can I be what I ought to be?" but the inventory of the new man is couched in faith and joy in his recognition that "Christ liveth in me!"

Paul expressed it to the Colossians in this way: "Christ in you, the hope of glory!" and then proceeded to assure them that "You are complete in Him!"

Paul wrote to the Ephesians to remind them that the essence of faith and hope in Christ is the assurance of being "accepted in the Beloved."

To the Corinthian believers, Paul promised full spiritual deliverance and stability in the knowledge that Jesus Christ "is made unto us wisdom, righteousness, sanctification and redemption."

Our great need, then, is simply Jesus Christ. He is what we need. He has what we need. He knows what we need to know. He has the ability to do in us what we cannot do—working in us that which is well-pleasing in God's sight.

This is a difficult point in spiritual doctrine and life for many people.

"What about my ambition? I have always been ambitious so it is a part of my being. Doesn't it matter?"

"I am used to doing my own thing in my own way—and I am still doing it in the church. Do I have to yield that?"

"I have always been able to put my best foot forward to get recognition and publicity. I am used to seeing my name in the paper. What do I get from crucifixion with Christ?"

Brothers and sisters, you get Christ and glory and fruitfulness and future and the world to come, whereof we speak, and the spirits of just men made perfect; you get Jesus, the mediator of a new covenant, and the blood of the everlasting covenant; an innumerable company of angels and the church of the firstborn and the New Jerusalem, the city of the living God!

And before you get all that, you have the privilege and the prospect of loving and joyful service for Christ and for mankind on this earth.

This is a gracious plan and provision for men and women in the kindness and wisdom of God. He loves you too well and too much to let you continue to strut and boast and cultivate your egotism and feed your *I*. He just cannot have that kind of selfish assertion in His children, so Jesus Christ works in us to complete Himself and make Himself anew in us.

So, you see, that is really why Jesus Christ came into this world to tabernacle with us, to die for us. God is never going to be done with us in shaping us and fashioning us as dear children of God until the day that we will see Him face to face, and His name shall be in our foreheads. In that day, we shall genuinely be like Him and we shall see Him as He is.

Truly, in that gracious day, our rejoicing will not be in the personal knowledge that He saved us from hell, but in the joyful knowledge that He was able to renew us, bringing the old self to an end, and creating within us the new man and the new self in which can be reproduced the beauty of the Son of God.

In the light of that provision, I think it is true that no Christian is where he ought to be spiritually until that beauty of the Lord Jesus Christ is being reproduced in daily Christian life.

I admit that there is necessarily a question of

degree in this kind of transformation of life and character.

Certainly there has never been a time in our human existence when we could look into our own being, and say: "Well, thank God, I see it is finished now. The Lord has signed the portrait. I see Jesus in myself!"

Nobody will say that—nobody!

Even though a person has become like Christ, he will not know it. He will be charitable and full of love and peace and grace and mercy and kindness and goodness and faithfulness—but he will not really know it because humility and meekness are also a part of the transformation of true godliness.

Even though he is plainly God's man and Christ's witness, he will be pressing on, asking folks to pray for him, reading his Bible with tears, and saying, "Oh, God, I want to be like Thy Son!"

God knows that dear child is coming into the likeness of His Son, and the angels know it, and the observing people around him know it, too. But he is so intent upon the will and desires of God for his life and personality that he does not know it, for true humility never looks in on itself. Emerson wrote that the eye that sees only itself is blind and that the eye is not to see with but to see through. If my eye should suddenly become conscious of itself, I would be a blind man.

Now, there is a practical application of the crucified life and its demands from day to day. John the Baptist realized it long ago when he said, "He must increase but I must decrease!"

There must necessarily be less and less of me—and more and more of Christ! That's where you feel the bite and the bitterness of the cross, brother! Judicially and potentially, I was crucified with Christ, and now God wants to make it actual. In actuality, it is not as simple as that. Your decision and commitment do not then allow you to come down from

131

that cross. Peace and power and fruitfulness can only increase according to our willingness to confess moment by moment, "It is no longer I, but Christ that liveth in me."

God is constantly calling for decisions among those in whom there is such great potential for displaying the life of Jesus Christ.

We must decide: "My way, or Christ's?"

Will I insist upon my own righteousness even while God is saying that it must be the righteousness of His Son?

Can I still live for my own honor and praise? No, it must be for Christ's honor and praise to be well-pleasing to God.

"Do I have any choice? Can I have my own plan?"

No, God can only be honored as we make our choices in Christ and live for the outworking of God's plan.

Modern theology refuses to press down very hard at this point, but we still are confronted often with spiritual choices in our hymnology. We often sing: "Oh, to be dead to myself, dear Lord; Oh, to be lost in Thee."

We sing the words, we soon shut the book, and drift away with friends to relax and have a pleasant soda. The principle does not become operative in most Christians. It does not become practical. That is why I keep saying and teaching and hoping that this principle which is objective truth will become subjective experience in Christian lives. For any professing Christian who dares to say, "Knowing the truth is enough for me; I do not want to mix it up with my day-to-day life and experience," Christianity has become nothing but a farce and a delusion!

It may surprise you that Aldous Huxley, often a critic of orthodox and evangelical Christianity, has been quoted as saying: "*My* kingdom *go* is the necessary correlary to *Thy* kingdom *come*."

How many Christians are there who pray every Sunday in church, "Thy kingdom come! Thy will be done!" without ever realizing the spiritual implications of such intercession? What are we praying for? Should we edit that prayer so that it becomes a confrontation: "My kingdom go, Lord; let Thy kingdom come!" Certainly His kingdom can never be realized in my life until my own selfish kingdom is deposed. It is when I resign, when I am no longer king of my domain that Jesus Christ will become king of my life.

Now, brethren, in confession, may I assure you that a Christian clergyman cannot follow any other route to spiritual victory and daily blessing than that which is prescribed so plainly in the Word of God. It is one thing for a minister to choose a powerful text, expound it and preach from it—it is quite something else for the minister to honestly and genuinely live forth the meaning of the Word from day to day. A clergyman is a man—and often he has a proud little kingdom of his own, a kingdom of position and often of pride and sometimes with power. Clergymen must wrestle with the spiritual implications of the crucified life just like everyone else, and to be thoroughgoing men of God and spiritual examples to the flock of God, they must die daily to the allurements of their own little kingdoms of position and prestige.

One of the greatest of the pre-reformation preachers in Germany was Johannes Tollar, certainly an evangelical before Luther's time. The story has been told that a devout layman, a farmer whose name was Nicholas, came down from the countryside, and implored Dr. Tollar to preach a sermon in the great church, dealing with the deeper Christian life based on spiritual union with Jesus Christ.

The following Sunday Dr. Tollar preached that sermon. It had 26 points, telling the people how to put away their sins and their selfishness in order to glorify Jesus Christ in their daily lives. It was a good sermon—actually, I have read it and I can underscore every line of it.

When the service was over and the crowd had dispersed, Nicholas came slowly down the aisle.

He said, "Pastor Tollar, that was a great sermon and I want to thank you for the truth which you presented. But I am troubled and I would like to make a comment, with your permission."

"Of course, and I would like to have your comment," the preacher said.

"Pastor, that was great spiritual truth that you brought to the people today, but I discern that you were preaching it to others as truth without having experienced the implications of deep spiritual principles in your own daily life," Nicholas told him. "You are not living in full identification with the death and resurrection of Jesus Christ. I could tell by the way you preached—I could tell!"

The learned and scholarly Dr. Tollar did not reply. But he was soon on his knees, seeking God in repentance and humiliation. For many weeks he did not take the pulpit to preach—earnestly seeking day after day the illumination of the Spirit of God in order that objective truth might become a deep and renewing and warming spiritual experience within.

After the long period of the dark sufferings in his soul, the day came when John Tollar's own kingdom was brought to an end and was replaced by God's kingdom. The great flood of the Spirit came in on his life and he returned to his parish and to his pulpit to become one of the greatest and most fervent and effective preachers of his generation. God's gracious blessings came—but Tollar first had to die. This is what Paul meant when he said, "I have been crucified with Christ."

This must become living reality for all of us who say we are interested in God's will for our lives. You pray for me and I will surely pray for you—because this is a matter in which we must follow our Lord!

We can quote this text from memory, but that is not enough. I can say that I know what Paul meant, but that is not enough. God promises to make it living reality in our lives the instant that we let our little, selfish kingdom go!

Chapter Ten

Christian, Do You Downgrade Yourself Too Much?

"Looking for that blessed hope, and the glorious appearing of the great God and our Saviour Jesus Christ; Who gave himself for us, that he might redeem us from all iniquity, and purify unto himself a peculiar people, zealous of good works."
Titus 2:13-14

The people of God, Christians who are living between the two mighty events of Christ's incarnation and His promised second coming, are not living in a vacuum!

It is amazing that segments in the Christian church that deny the possibility of the imminent return of the Lord Jesus accuse those who do believe in His soon coming of sitting around, twiddling their thumbs, looking at the sky, and blankly hoping for the best!

Nothing could be further from the truth. We live in the interim between His two appearances, but we do not live in a vacuum. We have much to do and little time in which to get it done!

Stretch your mind and consider some very apparent facts of our day.

Who are the Christians leaving all to staff the missionary posts around the world? Who are the

Christians staying at home and sacrificing in order to support the great evangelical thrust of the Christian gospel everywhere? Those who fervently believe that He is coming.

What kind of churches are busy praying and teaching and giving, preparing their young people for the ministry and for missionary work? Churches that are responding to Christ's appeal to "occupy until I come!"

Well, in this text Titus has given us Christian doctrine that has validity both in the light of the expected return of Jesus Christ as well as in the face of death.

It is in the record of the early Methodists in England, when there was persecution and testing in every direction, that John Wesley was able to say, "Our people die well!"

In more recent years, I have heard a quotation from a denominational bishop who estimated that only about ten per cent of the men and women in the membership of his church body are prepared and spiritually ready to die when their time comes.

I believe you can only die well when you have lived well, from a spiritual point of view. This doctrine of the Christian life and spiritual vitality of the believer as propounded by Titus has full validity in the face of any contingency which awaits us.

Titus quickly identifies Jesus Christ as the Saviour "who gave himself for us," and we can quickly learn the value of any object by the price which people are willing to pay for it. Perhaps I should qualify that—you may not learn the true value, for it is my private opinion that a diamond or other jewelry has no intrinsic value at all.

You may remember the story about the rooster scratching around in the barnyard for kernels of corn. Suddenly he scratched up a beautiful pearl of fabulous price which had been lost years before, but he just pushed it aside and kept on looking for corn.

The pearl had no value for the rooster, although it had a great value for those who had set a price upon it.

There are various kinds of markets in the world, and something which has no value for a disinterested person may be considered of great value by the person desiring it and purchasing it.

It is in this sense, then, that we learn how dear and precious we are to Christ by what He was willing to give for us.

I believe many Christians are tempted to downgrade themselves too much. I am not arguing against true humility and my word to you is this: Think as little of yourself as you want to, but always remember that our Lord Jesus Christ thought very highly of you—enough to give Himself for you in death and sacrifice.

If the devil does come to you and whispers that you are no good, don't argue with him. In fact, you may as well admit it, but then remind the devil: "Regardless of what you say about me, I must tell you how the Lord feels about me. He tells me that I am so valuable to Him that He gave Himself for me on the cross!"

So, the value is set by the price paid—and, in our case, the price paid was our Lord Himself!

The end that the Saviour had in view was that He might redeem us from all iniquity, that is, from the power and consequences of iniquity.

We often sing the words of a hymn by Charles Wesley in which the death of our Lord Jesus is described as "the double cure" for sin. I think many people sing the hymn without realizing what Wesley meant by the double cure.

"Be of sin the double cure, Save me from its wrath and power." The wrath of God against sin and then the power of sin in the human life—these both must be cured. Therefore, when He gave Himself for us, He redeemed us with a double cure, delivering us from the consequences of sin and delivering us from the power which sin exercises in human lives.

Now, Titus, in this great nugget of spiritual truth, reminds us that the redemptive Christ performs a purifying work in the people of God.

You will have to agree with me that one of the deep and outbroken diseases of this present world and society is impurity, and it displays itself in dozens of symptoms. We are prone to look upon certain lewd and indecent physical actions as the impurities which plague human life and society—but the actual lusting and scheming and planning and plotting come from a far deeper source of impurity within the very minds and innermost beings of sinful men and women.

If we were people of clean hands and pure hearts, we would be intent upon doing the things that please God. Impurity is not just a wrong action; impurity is the state of mind and heart and soul which is just the opposite of purity and wholeness.

Sexual misconduct is a symptom of the disease of impurity—but so is hatred. Pride and egotism, resentfulness and churlishness come to the surface out of sinful and impure minds and hearts, just as gluttony and slothfulness and self-indulgence do. All of these and countless others come to the surface as outward symptoms of the deep, inward disease of selfishness and sin.

Because this is a fact in life and experience, it is the spiritual work of Jesus Christ to purify His people by His own blood to rid them of this deep-lying disease. That is why He is called the Great Physician —He is able to heal us of this plague of impurity and iniquity, redeeming us from the consequences of our sins and purifying us from the presence of our sins.

Now, brethren, either this is true and realizable in human life and experience or Christianity is the cheap fraud of the day. Either it is true and a dependable spiritual option or we should fold up the Bible and put it away with other classical pieces of literature which have no particular validity in the face of death.

Thank God that there are millions who dare to stand as if in a great chorus and shout with me, "It is true! He did give Himself to redeem us from all iniquity and He does perform this purifying work in our lives day by day!"

The result of Christ's purifying work is the perfecting of God's very own people, referred to in this passage from the King James version as "a peculiar people."

Many of us know all too well that this word *peculiar* has been often used to cloak religious conduct both strange and irrational. People have been known to do rather weird things and then grin a self-conscious grin and say in half-hearted apology: "Well, we are a peculiar people!"

Anyone with a serious and honest concern for scriptural admonition and instruction could quickly learn that this English word *peculiar* in the language of 1611 describing the redeemed people of God had no connotation of queerness, ridiculousness nor foolishness.

The same word was first used in Exodus 19:5 when God said that Israel "shall be unto me a peculiar treasure above all people." It was God's way of emphasizing that His people would be to Him a treasure above all other treasures. In the etymological sense, it means "shut up to me as my special jewel."

Every loving mother and father has a good idea of what God meant. There are babies in houses up and down every street, as you can tell by the baby clothes hanging on the lines on a summer day.

But in the house where you live, there is one little infant in particular, and he is a peculiar treasure unto you above all others. It does not mean necessarily that he is prettier, but it does mean that he is the treasure above all other treasures and you would not trade him for any other child in the whole world. He is a *peculiar* treasure!

This gives us some idea, at least, of what we are—God's special jewels marked out for Him!

Titus then clearly spelled out one thing that will always characterize the children of God—the fact that they are zealous of good works.

Titus and all of the other writers who had a part in God's revelation through the scriptures agree at this point—our Lord never made provision for any of His followers to be "armchair" Christians. "Ivory tower" Christianity, an abstract kind of believing, composed simply of fine and beautiful thoughts, is not what Jesus taught at all.

The language in this passage is plain: The children of God in Jesus Christ, redeemed by the giving of Himself, purified and made unto Him as special jewels, a peculiar people, are characterized by one thing—their zeal for good works.

Because of the grace of God, we learn, these followers of Jesus Christ are zealous of good works and in their daily experience they live "looking." The Christian should always live in joyous anticipation of the blessed hope and the glorious appearing of the great God and our Saviour Jesus Christ!

Now, there is something in Christian theology that I want to share with you. Some people say they cannot bother with theology because they do not know either Greek or Hebrew. I cannot believe that there is any Christian who is so humble that he would insist that he knows nothing about theology.

Theology is the study of God and we have a very wonderful textbook—actually 66 textbooks rolled into one. We call it the Bible. The point I want to make is this: I have noted in study and in experience that the more vital and important any theological or doctrinal truth may be, the devil will fight it harder and bring greater controversy to bear upon it.

Consider the deity of Jesus, for example.

More and more people are arguing and debating and fighting over this absolutely vital and foundational truth.

The devil is smart enough not to waste his attacks on minor and non-vital aspects of Christian truth and teaching.

The devil will not cause any trouble for a preacher who is scared stiff of his congregation and worried about his job to the extent that he preaches for thirty minutes and the sum of what he says is "Be good and you will feel better!"

You can be as good as you want to and yet go to hell if you have not put your trust in Jesus Christ! The devil is not going to waste his time causing any trouble for the preacher whose only message is "Be good!"

But the believing Christian lives in joyful anticipation of the return of Jesus Christ and that is such an important segment of truth that the devil has always been geared up to fight it and ridicule it. One of his big successes is being able to get people to argue and get mad about the second coming— rather than looking and waiting for it.

Suppose a man has been overseas two or three years, away from his family. Suddenly a cable arrives for the family with the message, "My work completed here; I will be home today."

After some hours he arrives at the front door and finds the members of his family in turmoil. There had been a great argument as to whether he would arrive in the afternoon or evening. There had been arguments about what transportation he would be using. As a result, there were no little noses pushing against the window glass, no one looking to be able to catch the first glimpse of returning Daddy.

You may say, "That is only an illustration."

But what is the situation in the various segments

of the Christian community?

They are fighting with one another and glaring at each other. They are debating whether He is coming and how He is coming and they are busy using what they consider to be proof texts about the fall of Rome and the identification of the anti-Christ.

Brethren, that is the work of the devil—to make Christian people argue about the details of His coming so they will forget the most important thing. How many Christians are so confused and bewildered by the arguments that they have forgotten that the Saviour has purified unto Himself a peculiar people, expecting that we will live soberly, righteously and godly, looking for the glorious appearing of the great God and Saviour.

That is the Epiphany, which is an expression in the Christian church, and it is used in reference to Christ's manifestation in the world.

It is used in two senses in 1 Timothy and 2 Timothy.

First, Paul says in 2 Timothy 1:8-10: ". . . God, who hath saved us, and called us with an holy calling, not according to our works, but according to his own purpose and grace, which was given us in Christ Jesus before the world began, but is now made manifest by the appearing of our Saviour Jesus Christ, who hath abolished death, and hath brought life and immortality to light through the gospel."

In that passage we have the record of His first appearing, the shining forth when He came into the world to abolish death by His death and resurrection.

Then, the apostle in one of those moving and wonderful doxologies, said in 1 Timothy 6:13-16: "I give thee charge in the sight of God, who quickeneth all things, and before Christ Jesus, who before Pontius Pilate witnessed a good confession; that thou keep this commandment without spot, unrebukeable, until the appearing of our Lord Jesus Christ."

Paul speaks of the second appearing, when Christ

"shall shew, who is the blessed and only Potentate, the King of kings, and Lord of lords; Who only hath immortality, dwelling in the light which no man can approach unto; whom no man hath seen, nor can see: to whom be honour and power everlasting. Amen."

When I read something like this given us by the apostle Paul, it makes me think of a skylark or a meadowlark mounting a branch and bursting into an unexpected but brilliantly melodious song. Paul often breaks forth with one of his wonderful and uplifting ascriptions of praise to Jesus Christ in the midst of his epistles, and this is one of those!

Paul reminds Christian believers here that when Jesus Christ appears again, He will show forth, and leave no doubts at all, as to the Person of the King of kings and Lord of lords.

Paul was also careful to comfort those in the early church who feared that they might die before this second appearing of Jesus Christ. Actually, there were believers in the Thessalonian church who were worried on two counts, the first of which was their thought that the Lord had already come and they had been passed by. The second was their thought that they would die before He came and that through death, they would miss out on the joys of His appearing.

So, Paul wrote the two epistles to the Thessalonian church to straighten them out on the truth concerning Christ's second appearing.

"If we believe that Jesus died and rose again, even so them also which sleep in Jesus will God bring with him"—that is, if you die and go to be with the Lord, God will bring you along with Jesus at His appearing—"for this we say unto you by the word of the Lord, that we which are alive and remain unto the coming of the Lord shall not (run ahead of those) which are asleep. For the Lord himself shall descend from heaven with a shout, with the

144

voice of the archangel, and with the trump of God: and the dead in Christ shall rise first: Then we which are alive and remain shall be caught up together with them in the clouds, to meet the Lord in the air: and so shall we ever be with the Lord. Wherefore comfort one another with these words."

You see, Paul's inspired explanation instructs us that those who died before the coming of Jesus will not be at a disadvantage. If anything, they will be in a position of advantage, because before the Lord glorifies the waiting saints throughout the earth, He will raise in glorified bodies the great company of believers who have been parted from us by death throughout the centuries.

Brethren, that is very plainly what the apostle Paul tells us in the instructions originally given to the Thessalonian Christians.

Don't we have the right to think that it is very strange that the majority of the Christian pulpits are completely silent concerning this glorious truth of the imminent return of Jesus Christ? It is paradoxical that there should be this great silence in Christian churches at the very time when the danger of suddenly being swept off the face of the earth is greater than it has ever been.

Russia and the United States, the two great nuclear powers, continue to measure their ability to destroy in terms of *over-kill*. This is a terrible compound word never before used in the history of the English language. The scientists had to express the almost incredible destructive power of the nuclear bombs in our stockpiles—so the word *over-kill* is a new invention of our times.

Both the United States and Russia have made statements about the over-kill power of nuclear stockpiles sufficient to kill every man, woman and child in the world—not once, but 20 times over. That is over-kill!

Isn't it just like that old enemy, Satan, to persuade

the saints in the Body of Christ to engage in bitter arguments about post-tribulation rapture and pre-tribulation rapture; post-millennialism, a-millennialism and pre-millennialism—right at the very hour when over-kill hangs over us like a black, threatening cloud.

Brethren, this is the kind of age and hour when the Lord's people should be so alert to the hope and promise of His coming that they should get up every morning just like a child on Christmas morning—eager and believing that it should be today!

Instead of that kind of expectancy, what do we find throughout His church today? Arguments pro and con about His coming, about the details of the rapture—and some of this to the point of bitterness. Otherwise, we find great segments of Christians who seem to be able to blithely ignore the whole matter of the return of Jesus Christ.

Very few ministers bother to preach from the Book of Revelation any more—and that is true of large areas of evangelicalism and fundamentalism, too! We have been intimidated by the cynicism and sophistication of our day.

There are so many apparent anomalies and contradictions in society and in the ranks of professing Christians that someone will certainly write a book about it.

There is the anomaly of the necessity of getting to know one another better in order to love and understand one another better. Millions are traveling and meeting other millions and getting acquainted, so if the premise is true, we ought all to love each other like one big blessed family.

Instead, we hate each other like the devil. It is true that all over the world the nations are hating each other in startling, record-breaking measure.

I will mention another contradiction that is all too apparent. Our educators and sociologists told us that all we had to do was allow the teaching of sexual education in the schools and all of our vexing sexual problems in society would disappear.

Is it not a strange anomaly that the generation that has been teaching and outlining more about sexual practices than any twenty-five generations combined did in the past is the generation that is the most rotten and perverted in sexual conduct?

And is it not strange, too, that the very generation that might expect to be atomized suddenly by over-kill is the generation that is afraid to talk about the coming of the Lord and unwilling to discuss His gracious promises of deliverance and glorification?

You may not expect me to say it, but I will: what a bunch of weirdies we are! What a strange generation we are!

God has said that He would place a great premium on the holy, spiritual consistency of the Christian saints, but how inconsistent we are when we allow the devil and our own carnality to confuse and mix us up so that we will be diverted from patient waiting for His appearing!

So, we live between two mighty events—that of His incarnation, death and resurrection, and that of His ultimate appearing and the glorification of those He died to save. This is the interim time for the saints—but it is not a vacuum. He has given us much to do and He asks for our faithfulness.

In the meantime, we are zealous of good works, living soberly, righteously, godly in this present world, looking unto Him and His promise. In the midst of our lives, and between the two great mountain peaks of God's acts in the world, we look back and remember, and we look forward and hope! As members of His own loving fellowship, we break the bread and drink the wine. We sing His praise and we pray in His Name, remembering and expecting!

Brethren, that moves me more than anything else

in this world. It is such a blessed privilege that it is more beautiful and satisfying than friendships or paintings or sunsets or any other beauties of nature. Looking back to His grace and love; looking forward to His coming and glory; meanwhile actively working and joyously hoping—until He comes!

Chapter Eleven

Do You Love Your Lord, Never Having Seen Him?

"... Jesus Christ, whom having not seen, ye love..." 1 Peter 1:8

I think it may be safely said of the human family that it is possible to love someone we have never seen, but that it is totally impossible for us to love one whom we have not "experienced" in some way.

The apostle Peter, who had seen Jesus Christ in the flesh with his own eyes, passed along to every believing Christian the assurance that it is possible for us to love the Saviour and to live a life that will glorify Him even though we have not yet seen Him.

It is as though Peter is urging: "Love Him and work for Him and live for Him. I give you my testimony that it will be worth it all when you look upon His face—for I have seen Him with my own eyes, and I know!"

Once Peter was occupied with the chores of his fishing trade along the shores of Galilee as a quiet Man passed by, a Man with a marvelous magnetism, a glorious wonder about His face. When He flipped His pleasant finger at Peter, the big fisherman jumped up and followed and was in His company for three years.

Peter came to know personally the meaing of bit-

ter tears and strong weeping after his denial of the
Lord. I am sure he wept often when his thoughts
would sweep him along to the memories of the broken
body of the Messiah hanging on a cross. But his
eyes had also seen Jesus after He was risen from
the grave, for the Lord came forth and put His hand
on Peter's head and forgave him!

Peter had also seen Him before that in the glory
of the transfiguration—the preview of the glory that
awaited the Son of Man. Finally, Peter stood with
the other disciples as Jesus bade them farewell and
ascended into heaven from the Mount of Olives. All
of these were incidents in Peter's life which were
actual experiences in his relationship with the person
of Jesus Christ, his Lord and Master.

So, Peter had seen Jesus in the flesh, and was
moved to write to the strangers scattered abroad—
the Christians of the dispersion—to remind them that
they should love Jesus Christ even though they had
not seen Him in the flesh.

The Lord Jesus Himself had set His own stamp
of approval and blessing upon all Christians who
would believe, never having seen Him in the time
of His own flesh. He told Thomas after the resurrection, "Because thou hast seen me, thou hast believed:
blessed are they that have not seen, and yet have
believed."

I think it is a mistake for Christians to nurture
a kind of plaintive and pensive regret that they did
not live 2,000 years ago when Christ was upon the
earth. We are reminded of this attitude in a children's
hymn that most of us have sung at one time or another:

"I think when I read the sweet story of old,
How Jesus was here among men;
How He called little children as lambs to His fold,
I would like to have been with Him then."

I do not go on record as objecting to that song,

but I do not think it has any biblical authority. I truly believe that God has ordained that we may actually know Jesus now, and love Him better never having seen Him, than Peter did when he saw Him!

Now, about this matter of being able to "experience" others.

In our human race, some persons unfortunately are born without the ability to hear and others are born without the great gift of sight.

One who is born without the ability to hear may still know and experience and appreciate relatives and friends through the communication of the eyes.

One who is blind but has the faculty of hearing soon discovers the ability to experience and to come to know those who are around him by hearing their voices and learning all the sweet cadences of affection and love through the ears.

Even those who have had the double handicap of deafness and blindness have come to experience and know and appreciate other human beings—like Helen Keller, for instance, who learned to love people by feeling their faces with her sensitive fingers.

The story has been told that when Helen Keller was a young woman, she was introduced to the great tenor, Caruso. Unable to hear him, of course, she asked for the privilege of putting her fingers on his neck and chest bones while he sang one of his favorite operatic renditions. Her sensitive hands experienced the great range of the vibrations of his voice, and she stood as though transfixed. She could not hear his voice, but she experienced him in a most unusual way through the reading of her fingers.

I am sure it is true that we can love people we have not seen—but that it is impossible to love one whom we have not experienced in any way. It is a total impossibility for me to find any emotional response toward a person who has never come within the circle of my human experience.

For instance, do I love Abraham Lincoln?

Well, Abraham Lincoln is dead. I respect and admire his memory and I honor his great contributions to our nation and society. I believe he was a great man, but I feel no emotional response or personal human affection toward him.

If I had lived in the day of Lincoln and there had been opportunity for some correspondence between us, that opportunity to know and feel his great depth of personality would have certainly given me an emotional sense of affection and attachment. But as it is, I only know about Lincoln. I had no communication with him.

Actually, there have been people who confessed that they had fallen in love with another person through the writing of letters and the use of the mail. It is possible to experience others through the writing of letters—you get the pulse of them through the things they write and your imagination pieces it out and you may well experience love for the person of one whom you have not seen. It has happened.

God has seen fit to give us wonderful and mysterious faculties, and thus we human beings are able to know and experience and love someone we have not seen.

That is why Peter was able to witness to us of Jesus Christ and to tell us that we could and we should love Him, never having laid eyes upon His person in the flesh.

Notice that Peter did not assure us that we could love Jesus Christ without meeting Him in experience, in spirit, in His Word.

I think that one of the most hopeless tasks in the world is that of trying to create some love for Christ our Saviour among those who refuse and deny that there is a need for a definite spiritual experience of Jesus Christ in the human life.

I cannot understand the activities of many churches—their futile exercise of trying to whip up love and concern for Jesus Christ when there is no teaching of the new birth, no teaching of redemption through His blood, no dependence upon spiritual illumination by the Spirit of God!

No one can love the Lord Jesus Christ unless the Spirit of God is given opportunity to reveal Him in the life. No one can say that Jesus is Lord except the Holy Spirit enables him through spiritual life and experience.

Knowing this fact makes me question how any congregation can love and serve and glorify a Saviour whose very saviourhood is denied from the pulpit.

Peter writes that we are dedicated to the glory of the One whom we have not seen, because we love Him. That is the sum of Christianity—to know Him and to love Him!

"This is eternal life, that they might know me," Jesus taught. So, the knowledge of God is eternal life and the knowledge of setting forth the life of God in man is the business of the church.

It is a wonderful facet of love that we always take pleasure and delight in doing those things that are pleasing to the one we love. I find that the believing Christian who really loves his Lord is never irked or irritated in the service he is giving to Jesus Christ. The Lord will give him delight in true service for God—and I say it this way because generally the irksome and boring features of Christian service are some of the things that people and organizations have added on. I refer to things that have no scriptural validity.

It is always pleasant and delightful to set forth the praises of someone you really love. I think I see the illustration of that very often among the grandparents I meet, for they always whip out a wallet or a sheaf of pictures of their beautiful and talented grandchildren—whom they dearly love!

Those who truly love Jesus Christ find it one of the greatest pleasures in life to be able to simply describe how we discovered His great love for us, and how we are trying to return that love and devotion as we follow and serve Him in faith each day.

Now, Peter speaks out of a close relationship to Jesus, and in all of his writings speaks often of Jesus Christ, our Lord. He knew Jesus and had been instructed and taught of the Lord. There is reverence and dignity in his manner whenever he uses the name and titles of the Saviour.

Jesus was His name for Mary was told, "Thou shalt call his name Jesus because he is to be the Saviour of the world." The name Jesus had the same meaning as Joshua, which is "Jehovah saves."

Then, when Jesus went to the Jordan river and was anointed by the Holy Spirit, the title of Anointed One was His, which we express in the English language as Christ. This is His name and title—Jesus the Christ. Jesus, the Anointed One!

When Jesus Christ arose from the dead He took precedence over all creatures, whether in heaven or earth or hell. His exalted position in relation to all beings everywhere gave Him the title Lord, one who has the right and the power and the wisdom and the ability for sovereignty and dominion.

So, Jesus means Saviour. Christ means the Anointed One. Lord means just what it means in English—one who rightfully holds dominion, and, in this case, our Lord Jesus Christ is the One about whom the entire creation turns.

Now, before considering further the place of Jesus Christ in the creation, I want to remind you that the whole Bible and the complete life of the believing church also are wholly dependent upon God's final revelation of Himself in the person of Jesus Christ, His Son.

Our Lord Jesus Christ was that One who was with the Father and who was God and who is God and who was given the divinely-bestowed commission to set forth the mystery and the majesty and the wonder and the glory of the Godhead throughout the universe. It is more than an accident that both the Old and New Testaments comb heaven and earth for figures of speech or simile to set forth the wonder and glory of God.

The Son of God is described by almost every fair and worthy name in the creation. He is called the Sun of Righteousness with healing in His wings. He is called the Star that shone on Jacob. He is described as coming forth with His bride, clear as the moon. His Presence is likened unto the rain coming down upon the earth, bringing beauty and fruitfulness. He is pictured as the great sea and as the towering rock. He is likened to the strong cedars. A figure is used of Him as of a great eagle, going literally over the earth, looking down upon the wonders and beauties of lake and river and rock, of the mountains and the plains.

Brethren, you can be perfectly free to go to your Bible with assurance that you will find Jesus Christ everywhere in its pages. I am convinced that it was God's design that you should find the divine Creator, Redeemer and Lord whenever you search the scriptures, and you do not have to "read" anything into the Word that is not already there.

Where the person of Jesus Christ does not stand out tall and beautiful and commanding, as a pine tree against the sky, you will find Him behind the lattice, but stretching forth His hand. If He does not appear as the sun shining in his strength, He may be discerned in the reviving by the promised gentle rains falling from the heavens above.

I do not mind telling you that I have always found Jesus Christ beckoning to me throughout the scriptures. Do not be disturbed by those who say that Old Testament portions cannot be claimed by the Christian church. God has given us the Bible as a unit, and Jesus referred in His teachings to many Old Testament portions which foretold His person and His ministries.

For illustration, I would say that it would be very difficult for a man to live and function in a physical body that existed only from the waist up. He would be without some of the vital organs necessary for the sustenance of life.

Similarly, the Bible contains two parts of one organic revelation and it is divided so that the Old Testament is the Bible from the waist down and the New Testament is the Bible from the waist up. This may give an understanding to my expression that if we have one organic Bible and we cut it in two, we actually bleed it to death and we can, in effect, kill it by cutting it.

Let us read the Bible as the Word of God and never apologize for finding Jesus Christ throughout its pages, for Jesus Christ is what the Bible is all about!

As for the men who seem to be able to preach the Bible without finding Jesus Christ as the necessary way and truth and life, I can only comment that they are more blind than I ever thought it possible for anyone to be. Jesus Christ the Lord is the revelation from the Father—and His being has made God's written record for man both a necessity and a reality.

Now, in our day, the Christian church seems to have a variety of concerns, but in reality it has only one reason for being—and that is to show forth the life and mercy and grace of Jesus Christ. Study the relationship of the Body of Christ to Jesus Christ, its Head, and you soon realize that the life and witness and proclamation of the church is all about Jesus Christ.

You will understand that when I speak of the Christian church I am not speaking of any particular denomination. Christ's church is the church of the firstborn, purchased with His blood. Christ's church includes all twice-born believers who have been inducted into the kingdom of God by the operation of the Holy Spirit.

There is an example of what the church is all about in Acts 13. The believers had met together. They ministered unto the Lord and prayed. That is the chief concern and ministry of the Christian church, and it cancels out any question about the problem of "which denomination?"

Wherever you find the Lord Jesus Christ you will find the church. Our Lord Jesus and the company of His people—in that fellowship you find His church.

Years ago they described the teaching prowess of a certain well-known educator in this way: Put that accomplished teacher-communicator on one end of a log and a boy on the other—and instantly you had a college!

It is even more true that when Jesus Christ by His Spirit meets with two of His believing people, you have a church! You have it without any upkeep and without any overhead and without any elections. But Jesus Christ must be central and His Presence must be known among His people.

Some Christian groups seem to think that doctrine comes first. Doctrine is necessary to the understanding of Christ—but it will be a rather sad Christian group if it has only doctrinal emphasis and fails to recognize first of all the Presence of Jesus Christ. A church pleasing to Jesus Christ must be dedicated to honoring Him who shows forth the wonder and the glory of the Godhead.

Those who are engaged merely in ecclesiastical motions have missed the point—Jesus Christ Himself wants to be known and honored in the midst of His people, and this is what our life and fellowship is all about. Peter says it will be true above all in the midst of the church that we will honor and love Him, although we have not yet seen Him! In the Christian church, then, our objectives and our activities should only be those which scripturally point to the Lamb of God who takes away the sins of the world and which minister to the eternal welfare of men and women.

Now, let us consider the Person of Jesus Christ and His mandate from the Father in the creation of all things.

In a more relaxed generation, when people did not have to hustle and scurry to keep out of the way of automobile traffic, men would often go out and lie down under the stars, gaze up, and say: "What is man that Thou art mindful of him?" Now, it is hard to see through the smoke and the smog.

Modern man does occasionally halt long enough to think and wonder about the creation of the universe. With the use of one word in this passage, the word *whom*, referring to Jesus Christ, Peter gives the only possible answer—the creation is about *whom* —"Jesus Christ, *whom* having not seen, ye love."

The believing Christian who sees in the creation of all things the setting forth of the wonder and glory of Jesus Christ as Lord and Sovereign will have no more unholy days. He will no longer be inclined to divide existence between secular interests and holy interests. There is a divine sanctification of everything in his life when the believer fully realizes that God has made His creation as a garment to show forth the Lord Jesus Christ. I do not believe that any scientist or educator or anyone else can ever know or fathom the deep mysteries of creation without admitting that there is One *whom*—One who holds all things together in the vast universe, the One in whom all things cohere, as Paul told the Colossians.

Brethren, creation is the setting forth of Jesus Christ as Lord and Sovereign, for Jesus Christ is the purpose of God in creation! Let me urge you to go back and read again the first chapter of Ezekiel in which the man of God said, "I saw heaven opened, and I saw visions of God."

Ezekiel had a remarkable vision in which there were whirlwinds, great clouds, an unusual fire and brightness, and out of which came four living creatures, and the four had the face of a man, the face of a lion, the face of an ox and the face of an eagle.

Now, these living creatures coming out of the mysterious fire, it seems to me, stand for a heavenly and visible representation of the creation, and our Lord Jesus Christ, whom we have not yet seen, is the One that creation is all about.

Those strange creatures out of the fire show forth, in some measure, what our Lord Jesus Christ is like. The prophet saw the fourfold representation of the faces of a man, a lion, an ox and an eagle.

Years ago it was called to my attention that this fourfold division of the character of Jesus corresponds in a remarkable way to the presentation of His ministries recorded in the four Gospels.

This is not new to us by any means, but it is of great significance to students of the Word of God and to all who love our Lord Jesus Christ in truth.

Luke in his record clearly sets forth the emphasis upon the man, Jesus. Matthew sets Him forth as a lion and Mark, as an ox. John's record refers to His heavenly qualities, with the representation of the high-flying eagle.

Jesus was indeed a man and Luke's record seems suited particularly for the Greek culture which had long sought for perfection in manhood.

Matthew's record is intent upon its appeal to the Jewish heart and mind, giving emphasis to the messianic and kingly fulfillment of Jewish hopes in Jesus Christ, and thus the figure of the Lion of Judah.

Mark gives a brief, straight-from-the-shoulder record of Jesus, the man of action and power, a mighty worker. The representation in figure is that of the strength and faithfulness of the ox and the appeal, no doubt, was to the Roman mind and mentality of the day.

Coming to John's Gospel, we note a different emphasis. Luke had traced the genealogy back to Adam. Matthew had traced the ancestors of Jesus back to Abraham. But John goes back to the beginning of all things and appeals to all men and the whole world to consider the necessity for Jesus, the Divine Son of God, to become flesh and dwell among us.

John, in his record, insists that Jesus antedates all biography and all chronology, and he goes back to the beginning to set forth the wonder and the mystery and the glory of Jesus Christ. Let me tell you one of my fancies—something that I cannot actually prove.

I believe that there is a time coming in the plan of God when it will be plainly seen that all of the laws of nature and all of the beings that are in nature —beasts on the earth and fish that swim in the waters and birds that fly in the air, even tiny hoppers and creeping things that lisp their pitifully little note on the night breezes—are all necessary in setting forth even a little of the wonder of Jesus Christ!

You will recall that Jesus sent disciples to bring a little donkey for His use with the words, "Say that the Lord hath need of him." Even the sad-faced, comical, long-eared donkey was necessary to set forth the glory of the Messiah-Saviour on that day when the cries of "Hosannah" came from the admiring multitudes.

Now, I did not intend to say this, but I might as well make the application. I do not infer that there is any relation between the little beast and us, but I want to emphasize that many men and women have lost all sight of the fact that they are important to God. We are all important to God in setting forth the glory of the Lord Jesus Christ.

In a good sense, I want you to think more of

yourself. My appeal is that you should love Christ and then love yourself for Christ's sake, because you are important. It is not an accident of fate that God created you and redeemed you—if you are a Christian. Your Saviour and Lord does have need of you to show forth His glory and praise.

I thank God that the kingdom of God is not divided into areas for big, important people and areas for little, unimportant people. Every one is just as needful in God's sight as any other!

So, I conclude here with this idea: there are two levels on which Christians are living.

It has been revealed that animals have one level while angels live on a completely different level, and we human beings are a cross between angels and beast. We have bodies like the animals and we have souls like the angels above.

God has made us a little lower than the angels, but He has made us a little higher than the animals.

We have a body that came from the earth. But in that precious human body, the like of which our Lord yielded to a cross, we also have a spirit like unto that of the angels above. When God said we were made a little lower than the angels, He did not mean that He made our spiritual part lower than the angels—He did not! He made man's spiritual being higher than the angels, for that was made in the very image of God!

So, it is with these two levels of our human being that we look at Jesus. These human and physical eyes have never seen Him. These eyes that gaze out like the deer gazes out of the thicket—these eyes have not seen Him.

But we do love Him, do we not? Yes—and the reason is that there is another level, another part of us! There is the invisible, the eternal, inward and spiritual being, which has its own sight and its own vision, and with those eyes we have seen Him, known Him and loved Him.

Brethren, Peter encourages every Christian believer to know and serve and love Jesus Christ now, our understanding being enlightened through this inner spiritual sight He has given us! We live to show forth the honor of our God in Jesus Christ, until that gracious day of the Lord when we shall see Him face to face!

Chapter Twelve

Will There Be Any Lazy Folks in Heaven?

". . . and shewed me that great city, the holy Jerusalem, descending out of heaven from God, having the glory of God . . ." Revelation 21:10-11

Are you among those who hold the mistaken idea that there will be nothing to challenge you in the life to come? Are you among those who have read the account of the New Jerusalem, the City of God, and have wondered if it will be just a haven for the lazy and an endless gathering of bored and listless beings?

Let me refer you to the biblical doctrine of the image of God in man. I say this to you, sir, that apart from God Himself, the nearest thing to God is a human soul. And I promise you that in that Great Day you will not be without something to do, for God Himself is the great worker. He is the Creator —He is creative. All that He does is creative.

God did not create the heaven and the earth and all of the universe and then put a period after it, and write, "It is done—finale!" He is always creating. He has made us in His image. God is the great worker without limit, and we are the little workers with limit, or up to our limits, which we haven't found yet. But our creative powers will be in use.

Actually, one of the supreme glories of man is

his many-sidedness. He can be and do and engage in a variety of interests and activities. He is not fatally formed to be only one thing. A rock is formed to be a rock and it will be a rock until the heavens melt with fervent heat and the earth passes away. A star is made to shine and a star it ever will be. The mountain that pushes up into the sky has been a mountain since the last geological upheaval pushed it up there. Through all the years it has worn the garment of force on its back but it has always been a mountain—never anything else.

But man can be both cause and effect—he can be servant or master. He can be doer and thinker. He can be poet and philosopher. He can be like the angels to walk with God or like the beasts to walk the earth. Man is a many-faceted diamond to catch and reflect back the glory of the only God.

It is this versatility in the nature of man which has enabled him to enjoy both solitude and togetherness. If a human being is normal, he will need and enjoy both of these extremes.

Jesus said, "Enter into thy closet"—there is solitude.

The Apostle said, "Forsake not the assembling of yourselves together." There is society. These words, of course, were spoken to Christian believers, and it is true that every believing child of God is supposed to be able to enjoy, understand and appreciate both solitude and fellowship with others.

Every normal person must have time to be alone. He must have time and inclination to become acquainted with himself. He must become oriented to the universe in which he lives. He must have the blessing of quietness to send out his thoughts like flocks of obedient birds exploring the wonders of the universe. He must get acquainted with God and himself in the solitude of his own chamber.

But remember that there must always be a reaction for every action. As the moon must always wane after it waxes and the tide must always go out after it comes in, so mankind must have society as well as solitude.

After a time of loneliness and heart-searching and communion with the living God through His Spirit, a person must again seek the face of his fellowmen. God has meant it to be so. God has meant that we should be together in fellowship.

The fact is that God has made us for each other, and it is His will and desire that Christian believers should understand and appreciate one another.

Why, then, we ask, do we have such problems in our togetherness?

You cannot talk for five minutes about mankind without coming to the ugly, hissing word we call *sin*. It is sin, the disease of the human stream, that ruined everything. It is sin that has made us greedy, sin that has made us hate. Sin makes us lust for power, sin creates jealousy and envy and covetousness.

Anything that comes close to being peace in our society will be destroyed by the ravages of sin, and men without God and His grace and His will cannot know or attain to the gracious blessings of true peace.

But in the final state of humanity, in the final state of perfection minus all of the diseases of the mind and of the being, we will dwell in perfect enjoyment of each other's company and that will be the New Jerusalem, the holy city, that descends out of heaven from God.

It will be in that blessed society that we will truly appreciate one another and we will be recognized truly for what we are in Christ. In this present earthly order, it seems the one who gets attention and notice and appreciation is the noisy one or the aggressive one. Many worthy and splendid persons never have the opportunity to enrich the lives and friendship of others because they are quiet, self-effacing persons who will not push themselves to the front. Some others are handicapped by features that may not be considered attractive and others do not have a "winsome" personality. When will we humans learn that we lose the richness of many a rewarding personality because we are not more discerning and wiser?

But in that final consummation, when the City of God descends, we shall be able truly to appreciate each other. If it were not for the deadening and corroding effects of sin, the human soul would catch and reflect the light of God as diamonds catch and reflect the light of the sun, and we would know each other for we would see in each other something of the nature and beauty of God. God is infinite and without limit and through Him we could come to know one another without ever feeling "I am weary of him and bored with him."

We have assurance in the Word of God that in that day when the limitations of the flesh are removed and the negative qualities in our personalities are gone and the minor notes are all taken out of the symphony of personality, we will thank God for one another. We will know God better through one another as we find that we are simply prisms and lenses through which God shines. God shines in many ways throughout His universe, but I do believe that He shines best of all in the lives of men and women He created and then redeemed.

It is only sin that has cracked the lenses and distorted the image. It is only sin that has marred the vision and spoiled the picture, so that when we look at each other we do not see the true depth of potential.

When our Lord looked at us, He saw not only what we were—He was faithful in seeing what we could become! He took away the curse of being and gave us the glorious blessing of becoming. Scoffers say a man can only be what he is, but Jesus Christ said, "No, he is not what he is—but what he can become."

It is the Lord Jesus Christ who gives us the power to "become." John the Apostle sensed this in his words: "It doth not yet appear what we shall be, but we know that, when he shall appear, we shall be like him; for we shall see him as he is." It is the ability to become—to grow, to change, to develop, to move out to the edges of the perfection of human personality—that is the glory of the Christian life!

Therefore, in that day when the holy city descends, there will no longer be the blight of jealousy. No personality in that day will want to ensnare or enslave another. There will be no one with the spirit of war or force to march on another's domain, or make others subject to his greed. We will not suspect one another, there will be no arrests and there will be no courts in which to file a grudging complaint. Violence and murders will be gone and in that society all will fare graciously as one—there will be no slums and no ghettos and there will be no private compounds of the rich marked "No Trespassing."

Many wary humans have said, "The prospect is too good to be true!" But it is written, "I heard a great voice out of heaven saying, Behold, the tabernacle of God is with men, and he will dwell with them and they shall be his people. And God himself shall be with them, and they shall be his people, and God himself shall be with them, and be their God. And God shall wipe away all tears from their eyes; and there shall be no more death, neither sorrow, nor crying, neither shall there be any more pain: for the former things are passed away."

Anyone who has love and concern for the human race will say a quiet but fervent "Amen" to this prospect for the future with God and man dwelling together and with the former things—tears, sorrow, pain and death—having passed away.

We give credit to men in all ages of human history who have dreamed and longed for a perfect human society. They wanted to make the world a better place in which to live, but all have had to settle for a dream. All of their dreams and all of their utopian ideas have been spoiled and brought to naught by human forces of pride and prejudice, of selfishness and cynicism.

This world system in which we live can never be made perfect by a social regeneration based on man's own hopes and dreams, foibles and failures. We notice that the man who was in the Spirit on the Lord's day did not refer to social regeneration. He clearly and plainly said that this perfect, future world comes down out of heaven from God. Man's hopeless condition cannot be perfected by some slow process of social regeneration—it must be brought about through the miraculous process of individual regeneration.

Actually, there is really no such thing as "society." It is a word that reaches out and rakes in a whole world of ideas, but in truth, I am society, you are society, and the man next door and the boy that sells papers and the milkman and the mayor of the city and the president and the office boy that does the chores—that is society. It is the individual, actually, so when we try to put them together and call it society, we are building a false concept. We are likely to think of society as an organism, which it is not! Society is a name given to a great number of individual organisms.

It was for that reason that Jesus Christ rebuked completely any idea of the regeneration of human society when He came into this world. He said to a man, "You must be born again." He said, "Where two or three are gathered together in my name, there am I in the midst." He spoke of an individual and exclaimed, "One soul is of more value than all the world." Study the New Testament and you will find Jesus continually placed His emphasis upon the value and worth of the individual.

An individualist Himself, Jesus still plainly taught

168

that there would ultimately be a society of the blessed, an assembly of the saints, a happy gathering of the children of God. There would be a New Jerusalem with the spirits of just men made perfect. He promised many mansions in the Father's house where these individuals—regenerated—could come together and form that holy society.

It is impossible to talk to people about blessedness and holiness and heaven without talking about God's provision of spiritual transformation. Everyone knows there are worldwide forces in our day which emphasize nationalism to the point that the individual is completely forgotten—but the only regeneration known in the entire world is individual regeneration. Many church groups seem to have joined forces with the political and social reformers in the dream that the effective way to bring about a perfect society is to reform and redeem society itself—rather than the redemption of the individual human natures which compose society, so-called.

What does the Bible say? It says there will not be one soul, not one member of that heavenly population, that will not have experienced the mystical and mysterious and spiritual regeneration of the new birth in some way, somewhere, during the brief earthly existence. It must be said of him, as Paul said of the new man in Christ, "Old things have passed away; all things have become new."

It is more than coincidence, then, that we find the same thing said about the New Jerusalem: "Old things have passed away; lo, I make all things new!"

How is it that the Holy Ghost said the same thing about the New Jerusalem that He had said about the converted man? Because the New Jerusalem will be the city of the converted man! This New Jerusalem will be filled with those who can say while they are on earth: "Old things have passed away, and all things have become new!" And then they will be able also to say: "He makes all things new, and the former things have passed away!''

God Himself will have a gracious plan for everyone in that great and eternal and holy city—and it will be a city that will satisfy all of man's nature.

I find that many men and women are troubled by the thought that they are too small and inconsequential in the scheme of things. But that is not our real trouble—we are actually too big and too complex, for God made us in His image and we are too big to be satisfied with what the world offers us!

Augustine put it in classical language when he said, "O God, Thou hast made us for Thyself, and our hearts are dissatisfied until they find their rest in Thee." That expression has been echoed and reechoed and written into our hymns, because it is true! Man is bored, because he is too big to be happy with that which sin is giving him. God has made him too great, his potential is too mighty. People do not actually commit suicide because they are too little and insignificant, but because they are big in a little world. God made man to be able to enjoy all of the vast expanses of His heaven and they have been forced through sin to be satisfied with paying their taxes and mowing the lawn and fixing the car and keeping the kids out of jail and paying their debts—yes, and getting older every day! They are sick of it, actually sick of it! Their bodies are breaking down and their tabernacle is too small for the spirit that dwells within.

That is the reason why humans are always trying to explore some new place. That explains the interest in trying to visit the moon. That explains why we want to be able to travel faster than sound. It explains, at least in part, why Charles Lindbergh jumped in an old egg-beater and was the first man to fly alone over the ocean to Paris. It explains why Admiral Byrd went down to the Antarctic and Admundsen explored the North Pole region. It is the reason for men always trying to do the impossible. It explains why we explore the secrets of the universe and come up with the atomic bomb—men are too big for the little world that sin has given them!

But the society that God is promising from above, that great City of God, will truly satisfy man's full nature. The day will be a long golden day without a cloud and without a sundown. Travel where you will in all those wide regions above and you will not find a wrinkle on anyone's face nor a gray hair on anyone's head. You will never hear anyone mutter, "I am discontented." You will never hear a voice raised in criticism. You will never meet a peevish man and you will never see an unkind face. You will never hear a growl from any throat, never a scream of fear or pain. You will never see a tear running down anyone's cheek.

Someone will break in here and say, "Just a minute, Mr. Tozer! That is the old-fashioned idea of heaven, where we are kind of glorified butterflies waving our wings gently in the zephyrs that flow down from the celestial mountains. What about a challenge? What about something to work for? How will the redeemed be occupied?"

Well, I can set you right there, because God promised that in the New Jerusalem He has provided all that is good and blessed and useful and has ruled out and barred only those things that offend.

When God put Adam and Eve in the garden, He did not put them there to sit and look at each other and to hold hands. He said they were to take care of the garden. You remember that—they were given something to do. Some people believe that work is a result of the curse, but that's not true. The idea is abroad that the man who works is a boob, and that work is only for fools—but God made us to work.

You know, the anthropologists say that when God made man with his four fingers and his thumb opposite those four fingers so that he could hold and use every kind of tool and instrument, He guaranteed that man would conquer the world. God made you and me like that, you see. So, sometime when you have a little time alone, look at that hand of yours, that amazing hand of yours!

The plain truth is that in all the machinery and all the gadgets and all the instruments around your house put together there is nothing that can remotely compare with the intricacy, beauty of performance and versatility of that right hand of yours. And God did not give you that hand to hang on to some chandelier in the New Jerusalem—God means that you are to go to work up there.

But it will be a tireless work—it will not be a work of boredom. It will be happy, joyous work. It will be work without fatigue. I do not know what God will have us doing. Maybe He will have you doing something that you can do.

"Our Lord was a worker," says one of our hymns, and our Lord is always looking for workers. So we are all going to be workers, and you need not imagine for a second that you will have nothing to do in heaven.

But along with work, heaven is also a place for you to rest.

You say, "How can you make these two statements agree?"

Well, you will work and you will not be tired. Jesus now works but without tiring. He rests always while He works. So the saints of God will work.

What was that which Kipling said?

"When earth's last picture is painted, and the tubes are twisted and dried; the brightest colors have faded and the youngest critic has died; we shall rest and they that need it shall lie down for an aeon or two; and the Master of all good workmen shall put us to work anew."

Kipling goes on to say, "We'll sit in a golden chair

and splash on a ten-league canvas with brushes of angel hair."

I do not know whether angels have hair—Kipling thought so. He thought it was a nice thing to do—to use a ten-league canvas instead of a miniature and sit there and work.

I think in that sense Kipling was right—heaven is not going to be a haven for lazy bums. Heaven is going to be a place where men released from tensions and inhibitions, released from prohibitions from the outside, released from sin, and made in the image of God can go to work like the young gods they are. For He said, "Ye are gods"—He didn't mean you are God, but "You are little images of mine, born to do the kind of work I do, creative work."

So, the New Jerusalem will be fresh opportunity for all of the imaginative and the industrious and the busy—who, like God, must find expression.

Ah, the beauty of it all—how can I go on? The beauty of it—not the done-up beauty of a woman's face, not the beauty of a carefully-padded form, not the beauty of the primrose that smiles in the sunshine, but the great, rich, strong beauty of eternity in God. Ah, that city of gold, with all its beauty!

Way back there in the beginning, God made man to live with Him. Sin came and God divorced man like an unfaithful wife from His presence. But through the miracle of redemption, through the cross of Jesus Christ, man is reborn back to his ancient place and raised yet above that.

Now, why was there no mention here of a temple, a church, a synagogue? Why was there no meeting place for worshipers?

Because all of that new City of God was a temple. God Himself was the temple. Like a great expanse of beautiful arches, the Father, Son and Holy Ghost surrounded and settled down and mingled with all of that carefree, busy, joyous throng. There they do not have to wait for an hour in which to pray—all hours are prayer hours there.

You won't have to wait to go to a special place to pray there—all of it is a temple and God and the Lamb are the temples thereof. There's no need for an artificial light to brighten the night, for the Lamb is the light thereof.

We must seriously consider whether we are headed in that direction. Every one of us must seriously consider whether we have—by the blood of the Lamb and the word of our testimony—overcome and escaped from the thralldom of sin, or whether we are still bound by it, cursed with the curse, and about to be destroyed in the destruction.

This is the gracious reality of our look to the future: We are by faith the children of God, given a place in that great society of the ransomed and promised an eternal inheritance in that Great City because our names are written in the Lamb's Book of Life!